EV 4.00

YO-CBB-908

Parenting the Other Chick's Eggs

Written by
Ruth-Ann Clurman

Edited by National Press Publications

NATIONAL PRESS PUBLICATIONS
A Division of Rockhurst College Continuing Education Center, Inc.
6901 W. 63rd St. • P.O. Box 2949 • Shawnee Mission, Kansas 66201-1349
1-800-258-7248 • 1-913-432-7757

Parenting the Other Chick's Eggs
© 1997, Ruth-Ann Clurman
Published by National Press Publications
A Division of Rockhurst College Continuing Education Center, Inc.

Printed in the United States of America.

1 2 3 4 5 6 7 8 9 10

ISBN #1-55852-175-5

About Rockhurst College
Continuing Education Center, Inc.

Rockhurst College Continuing Education Center, Inc., is committed to providing lifelong learning opportunities through the integration of innovative education and training.

National Seminars Group, a division of Rockhurst College Continuing Education Center, Inc., has its finger on the pulse of America's business community. We've trained more than two million people in every imaginable occupation to be more productive and to advance their careers. Along the way, we've learned a few things. Like what it takes to be successful ... how to build the skills to make it happen ... and how to translate learning into results. Millions of people from thousands of companies around the world turn to National Seminars for training solutions.

National Press Publications is our product and publishing division. We offer a complete line of the finest self-study and continuing-learning resources available anywhere. These products present our industry-acclaimed curriculum and training expertise in a concise, action-oriented format you can put to work right away. Packed with real-world strategies and hands-on techniques, these resources are guaranteed to help you meet the career and personal challenges you face every day.

Acknowledgments

A book is never authored by just one person. It takes a team of individuals dedicated to playing the roles they choose or happen to be assigned.

Marilyn Shapiro shepherded me through the UMKC Law Library and made it seem less a maze and more a research option.

Amy Winterscheidt was wildly enthusiastic when I showed her my title one day and asked, "What do you think?"

Deborah Shouse continues to encourage me and was the first and best source of information about "How do you write a book?" She is a remarkable cheerleader!

Anne Baber offered her ear and her writing and publishing experience.

Barbara Ann Pachter shared wisdom, consultation, friendship and empathy for the stepparenting experience.

Jim and Ruth Siress have encouraged, offered ideas and material, and answered desperate phone calls even when they were busy.

My friends Sheila and Sharon have endured my moods, listened to my frustration and never said, "Will you get this done, already? You have been working on it for three years!"

Steve, Cameron, Ross and Stephanie are my living laboratory and never complain about being guinea pigs.

Thank you to the countless people in my stepparenting workshops and in my seminars who have said, "When is the book going to be ready? I really need it!"

Thank you Sheryl Trick and Lynn Wilson who have listened to panicky phone calls, had infinite patience, and helped make this book happen.

Thank you Recie Mobley, Sharon Yoder and Gary Weinberg who listened, had faith and made publication possible.

Dedication

To Steve, who got me into this stepparenting adventure! His support, frustration, determination and love for each of us has helped us learn from each other, love each other and grow together.

To my parents, Helen and Ward Lawrence, who actively and lovingly parented and set the parenting example I try to follow.

To my grandmother Bernson, who always made me feel important, even when I was "just a kid." I learned from her that kids are people too.

To My Stepchildren

Before you came into my life,
there was an emptiness I was not even aware of.

I was spending my life priding myself on living it well.
I was complimenting me on my life
without the complications, frustrations and pains
I saw in people who had children.

But you erupted into my life,
complicating it and causing me endless pain
and frustration ...
and you have shown me a priceless piece of my heart
that I was unconsciously longing to know.

Without you, Cameron, I would never have known
that tears could accompany a first home run.
Without you, Ross, I would never have felt
the throat-clenching joy of hearing a choir of children sing.
Without you, Stephanie, I would never have experienced
the tenderness of attempting to answer childhood questions.

Without each of you,
I would be sleepwalking through pieces of my life,
unaware that what I viewed as nightmares
could fulfill unrealized dreams.

I thank you for the love you have awakened in me
and allowed me to experience.

Legend Symbol Guide

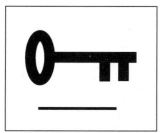

Key issues to learn and understand for future application.

Questions that will help you apply the critical points to your situation.

Checklist that will help you identify important issues for future application.

Exercises

"Chicks" Glossary

Let's get serious for a minute. Some of the "Chicks" terminology may befundle you from time to time. This glossary should help you decipher some of it.

Eggs... The Kids

Chick (Bio or Step): .... The mom

Rooster (Bio or Step): ....The dad

Nest/Henhouse/Coop: .... The home

Flock/Aviary: ....The whole family

Yard: ....The extended families and society at large

Pecking:.. Conflict/fighting

Clucking: .... Communication

Grain/Seedlings: .... Food

CONTENTS

I NTRODUCTION

How to Read This Book
(The Keys to the Chickenyard)

The Decline of the Chickenyard as We Knew It

By the year 2000, the stepfamily will be the most common form of family in the United States. We have lost the innocence of the "ideal," biologically intact family. But that "ideal" family was always more of a storybook fantasy than a day-to-day reality.

In the real world of families, biologically intact and blended, we step in a lot of what covers the dirt of a chickenyard or is found on the floor of a chickenhouse. We can cry with Chicken Little, "The sky is falling," or we can put on our boots and step boldly into this unknown coop we willingly entered. We can look around and begin the greatest experiment of our lives.

Breed Resistance to Those Crying "Fowl"

We are creating a hybrid, constructing a new nest. Does that word "hybrid" fit us? The dictionary defines hybrid as: "animals or plants of mixed origin." I think we've got it! The dictionary also provides "mongrel" as a synonym.

Much of the chickenyard would like to define us as mongrels. We get little encouragement from the yardbirds who observe us

> *"Perhaps all the dragons of our lives are princesses who are only waiting to see us once beautiful and brave."*
>
> Ranier Maria Rilke

> *"No snowflake ever falls in the wrong place."*
>
> Zen

and comment. Hens stare at us clucking while roosters shake their heads, squawk and throw dirt around.

In this nest, we certainly agree that we are of mixed origin, but we are determined to face this new experience with a willingness to confront new beings unlike ourselves. We will create a hybrid resistant to the feather-rufflers in the yard. Our nest will be a comfortable nest which makes room for each bird, no matter what it looks like. We will come out of this experience crowing rather than clucking or squawking.

Strutting Through the "Stuff"

We are in this game to play because we cannot afford to lose. We do not want to become a negative statistic in this yard, and we refuse to accept all that "stuff" on the floor of the yard as our reality. We will fly to a nest which we have made orderly and livable, feathering it with our sense of humor, our zest for life and our appreciation of the unfamiliar.

We will face the occasional unexpected nest-construction difficulties and deal with the unpleasant members of the yard at large.

Will This Flock Ever Learn to Fly?

"Where do we begin construction?"
"How do we continue it?"

"Who's got the blueprints for the nest?"
"Do blueprints exist?"

"Can we start without the blueprints?"
"Who can start without blueprints?"

"Does the construction get easier?"
"Does it get harder?"

"What role do I play in construction?"
"Am I the only one building? Why don't the others build?"

Any of these thoughts or questions sound familiar?

Are you:

- Desperate?

- Seeking help?

- Just reading this because you read everything you can find about stepparenting?

- Doing well in your stepfamily but always interested in a new idea or an enhancement for an old one?

In any or all of these cases plus many more, you have come to the right chickenyard.

What Help Can the Flock Find Here?

1. Positive attitudes and information about this hybrid
2. Real nest-construction tips
3. Action ideas for blending this interesting group of birds
4. Suggestions for dealing with the chickenyard at large
5. Hope that this hybrid will survive

The nest-construction tips found here are constructive even as:

- The eggs run wild.

- The unsolicited advice from the coop rains down.

- The yard screams doom to your hybrid.

- The exchicks or exrooster and their extended families plot and pray for your failure.

Negatives and "why your nest plans will fail" information with all the details about the exchick and exrooster's behavior are all around you. You don't need to read them here. You are living them.

> *"When I sit down to make a sketch from nature, the first thing I do is, to forget that I have ever seen a picture."*
>
> John Constable

These Nesting Blueprints Will...

1. Bring you sanity by helping you determine structure.
2. Help your running-amuck emotions find direction.
3. Provide options for the construction which best fits your group.
4. Give reinforcement for many things you have done right.
5. Present "Aha's" when you read the blueprint and think, "Why didn't we think of that?" That will make this construction much easier!
6. Cause you to say, "Let's not get depressed, let's get going (and in the same direction this time).

How Can the Experiences of the Clurman Coop Help?

This book was born out of my frustration in trying to deal with coop diseases, nest-wrecking attempts from the yard, wild eggs, an unhappy rooster and a chick about to flee the coop who was not able to find a clear, positive, how-to-do-it source of information.

Since I couldn't find the book I needed, after the experiences we had living in the nest, I decided to write it. I can't promise to have described every conceivable problem your nest might encounter, but I've covered many of the problems we blended nests have in common.

There Can Be Room for Everyone in the Nest

The Clurman Coop began as a group of people not too pleased about being stuck in the same chickenyard, much less in the same nest. We have evolved into a group of people who are crazy about the yard, coop, nest and all the bird inhabitants (of the nuclear nest, that is).

Some of our construction successes have been by conscious nest-blueprint design and some by accidental occurrence. We share our stories and experiments in wonder and gratefulness and in the hope that some of our suggestions will help your flock make your nest more comfortable.

How Do You Adapt Our Suggestions to Fit Your Nest?

1. Read with an open mind. (Forget the "stuff" in your yard.)
2. Read with an "I'll find a way to make this work in our nest" attitude.
3. Read to the eggs who can't read for themselves, and ask them the questions they can understand.
4. Begin the nest construction or reconstruction even when some members are determined not to build.
5. Nest members who don't want to participate will benefit from the changed attitudes of those who choose to participate.
6. Participating birds will have reduced stress because they will have a more comfortable place in the nest.

"There is an alternative. There's always a third way, and it's not a combination of the other two ways. It's a different way."

David Carradine

Hybrids Can Produce Stronger Breeds

You are about to become a part of, or are now a part of, a giant chickenyard which has been described as "a melting pot with enough heat to do the melting."

To change our nest, we had to learn that sometimes what we did best together was struggle for space and position. Our nest was not perfect according to some observers, but we worked hard to create a working, loving chickenyard. Our coop, with its shared sorrows, unexpected joys, realistic hopes and reformulated blueprints has become a place which nurtures us and those who come into contact with us.

This new kind of hybrid flock will move forward into the 21st century, accepting the special and challenging mission of continuing to create and revise blueprints about what this flock can be and accomplish.

We will say with Theodore Roethke, "What we need is more people who specialize in the impossible." Don't listen to the cluckers, flappers and squawkers. Fight and scratch to make what the yard tells you is impossible a reality. With time, caring and hard work, your nest can produce golden eggs!

CHAPTER 1

Planning the Nest

"I don't have a clue. Do you?"

"The way you house your chickens influences their state of health. No matter how you choose to house your chickens, they need protection from cold, heat, rain, wind and predators."

from *The Chicken Health Handbook*

Ralph Waldo Emerson's words "Nothing great was ever achieved without enthusiasm" are true. It takes a great deal more than enthusiasm to make a stepfamily a success. Planning is an essential part of successful nest construction.

> *"But the breathtaking part of it all was not so much the planning as the fantastic skill with which the planning was concealed."*
>
> Eva Le Gallienne

The Nest Gets Off to a Shaky Start Without Careful Planning

Two sets of eyes peered through the glass on the door of my apartment building. Small hands, foreheads and noses were pressed tightly to the glass. Suddenly the cry went up, "It's a girl, Dad!" Steve had told his sons that they were picking up a friend to go to the ball game with them. As the boys realized that this wasn't "just a friend," they giggled nervously. When I opened the door, Cam punched Ross and endeared himself to me quickly by saying, "She's pretty, Dad."

As I walked down the stairs that day, I had emotions tumbling over each other. I was telling myself, "I've taught school for seventeen years. I've never met a kid I didn't like. Kids have always liked me." I was carefully considering my conscious choice not to have children in my first marriage. I had all the kids I wanted at school and had never felt the need or desire to bring any of them home with me on a full-time basis. Now I was facing the possibility that having decided not to have my own, I might be raising someone else's. The thought was not entirely thrilling.

I looked at those two faces pressed against the glass and the bodies jumping up and down as they saw me and had to chuckle to myself. These are just two little boys. Why am I so nervous? I have since had ample time to learn why I was so afraid.

After my first marriage, I had determined not to marry again. Who needs the hassle? I was the happiest single person I have ever known. But out of the blue, I had met this man and was falling in love. I couldn't meet someone with no complications. No, I had to meet someone with three young, lively children. Now what?

I never really considered not marrying Steve because of the kids, but they were also the three best reasons not to marry him. Each time a member of the chickenyard at large offered advice, solicited or otherwise, I was told, "Those kids are going to be the reason you fail, if you do. It's tough to make a marriage work when kids and exes are involved."

In spite of the demoralizing words of yardbirds, I thought, as each of us do, "It will be different for us. We will be a great, happy nest. I have all this experience with other people's eggs. This won't be tough. We'll be scrambled into the same casserole and blending perfectly in no time."

Then I met Steph. An independent, honest child, the baby of the family who at five years of age blurted out, "You're not my boss!" She was simply vocalizing the tension, uncertainty and fright of each of us. We didn't know what was going to happen, and we didn't know how to influence what was happening. We needed serious planning in order to keep from pushing each other out of the nest.

Even knowing we needed planning there never seemed to be time, what with wedding preparations, a nest to buy, checking accounts to change and chickenyards to meet. Once again, we reverted to the, "It will all work itself out after the wedding," thinking. Happily-ever-after nest thinking has been the road to unhappiness for many a flock.

You would not attempt to build your house without careful planning. You would enlist those who are construction experts to help you plan. You would consult architects, engineers, realtors, interior designers and many more to be certain that this life investment would really pay off.

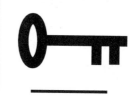

Some of your goals would be:
- to have a desirable living space
- to meet the needs of your unique group of family members
- to have a comfortable space for all to live
- to have a warm environment to entertain friends and extended family

Before attempting to design a house which would make you happy and meet your needs, the experts would ask you many questions about:
- the needs of your family
- your likes and dislikes
- your past experiences
- your comfort zones

"Make no little plans. They have no magic to stir men's blood. Make big plans: aim high in hope and work."

D.H. Burnham

So much planning, so much time to have a living space that enhances your growth and development as individuals and as a group.

Yet, as stepfamilies, we often attempt to build homes without any kind of organized planning. We want the same things in our family that we would want in our house:
- a desirable living space
- to meet the needs of our family members
- to create a warm living environment for family and friends

We sometimes just don't realize how to get these things.

You may try to consult experts. You read books and articles. In those books and articles you find horror stories about stepparenting and suggestions that there's really no way to build a successful stepfamily structure. You find the "whats" of things to do but seldom the "how-to's."

When you talk to other flocks about how to design your nest, you get the nest-wrecking stories first and are basically left with the impression that anything good that may happen will simply be miraculous.

So you go back to the comfort of your cloud-like fantasies and "happily ever after" thoughts. Research and blueprint design are nightmares, and you don't want to think that this experience is going to be a nightmare. You hope for a dream.

"It's a bad plan that admits of no modification."

Publilius Syrus

Building This Nest Will Be Fun

One of the moms/stepmoms I interviewed for this book put it like this: "We were thinking, 'We are so much in love. This is incredible! We have to hurry, get married and get started in this family. We thought the kids would fall in love with us and our new family the way we fell in love with each other.' We thought they would say, 'This is the happiest thing that has ever happened!' "

You feel that constructing a nest should be a pleasant experience. You know lots of work will be involved, but you're also excited about how wonderful things will be when you have created this new environment.

If you're reading this book at the beginning of your construction or after many cracked and scrambled-egg experiences, there's still time to design a blueprint and remodel.

If you're reading this book considering a stepfamily experience, you're ahead of most, who simply jump into the nest and hope it will be comfortable. When we hope for the best without planning, eggs get crushed, roosters fight and hens scratch. There are no existing blueprints for this nest. Using the tools in this chapter, you will be able to construct your own blueprint.

So, those who are about to begin this adventure will be asking, "Is there room in the nest for all of us?" And those who are already in the nest will be asking, "How can it get more comfortable in here?" Let's build the foundation for a successful living space.

Get a Flock History

Your blueprint design will include using yourselves as the experts on:
- You and what you need
- Your likes and dislikes
- Your past experiences
- Your comfort zones

The flock history needs to begin with the history of the rooster and the hen. Emily and John Visher point out in their book *Stepfamilies: Myths and Realities*, "In a recent study of family functioning, Jerry Lewis and colleagues report that one very important dimension in psychologically healthy families is the cohesiveness of the couple in the family. If the relationship between the spouses is strong and withstands attempts by the children to split or weaken the alliance, the family unit is able to cope successfully."

Who are we separately and who do we want to be together? In order to design a new nest, we need to be aware of:
- The nests we now inhabit which feel comfortable
- The history of those nests

So, the first piece of work for the couple whatever stage you find yourselves is to examine the nests you now have.

"Particulars are not to be examined till the whole has been surveyed."

Emanuel Celler

> *"Hope nothing from luck, and the probability is that you will be so prepared, forewarned and forearmed, that all shallow observers will call you lucky."*
>
> Edward George Bulwer-Lytton

Worksheet Purpose:

This worksheet will help you get a history of your separate nests so that a new one can be built successfully.

Worksheet Directions:

1. Each of you should fill out this worksheet independently of the other.

2. Together, agree on a deadline date for finishing the worksheet.

3. Fill it out when you have some time to think.

4. Sit down with your cup of coffee or tea and fill it out in a relaxed way.

5. Don't hurry or belabor the process. (Sometimes the most accurate answer is the one you think of first.)

6. After each of you has filled out the worksheet, make a "date" to read each other's sheet. This should also be done in a comfortable, relaxed environment.

7. Create an open atmosphere, where you can go through each question one by one and ask questions and discuss answers.

Nest History

1. In my experience, the most important responsibility of egg-parenting is ...

_____

_____

_____

_____

_____

2. Being a parent involves ...

_____
_____
_____
_____
_____

3. The thing I disliked most about my ex-nestmate was ...

_____
_____
_____
_____
_____

4. The thing I liked most about my ex-nestmate was ...

_____
_____
_____
_____
_____

5. The discipline in my childhood family was ...

_____
_____
_____
_____
_____

6. The thing I liked most about the way my parents raised me was ...

_____
_____
_____
_____
_____

"He who every morning plans the transaction of the day and follows out that plan carries a thread that will guide him through the maze of the most busy life. But where no plan is laid, where the disposal of time is surrendered merely to the chance of incidence, chaos will soon reign."

Victor Hugo

7. The thing I liked least about the way my parents raised me was ...

_____
_____
_____
_____
_____

8. How did your childhood nest/previous nest celebrate birthdays?

_____
_____
_____
_____
_____

9. What holidays were important in your childhood nest?

_____
_____
_____
_____
_____

10. Did you decorate for holidays in your childhood nest/previous nest? How much?

_____
_____
_____
_____
_____

11. Did you spend holidays with the extended chickenyard in your childhood nest/previous nest?

_____
_____
_____
_____
_____

"One cannot plan too carefully, but it is well to do this disinterestedly, as if you were planning for someone else, not committing yourself to execution nor drawing in advance upon that fund of emotion which you will need when you come to act. There are no such wastes as those of the anticipative imagination."

Charles Horton Cooley

12. Are there ways in which you wish holidays, birthdays, festivities had been handled differently in your childhood nest/previous nest?

_____

_____

_____

_____

_____

13. What other times of celebration besides birthdays and holidays do you feel are important nest-bonding times?

_____

_____

_____

_____

_____

14. What kind of relationship do you want with your ex-nestmate?

_____

_____

_____

_____

_____

15. If you could change some points of your divorce agreement, what points would you change?

_____

_____

_____

_____

_____

16. What manners do you feel are important to teach eggs?

_____

_____

_____

_____

_____

17. How important was religion or faith in your childhood nest/ previous nest?

_____

_____

_____

_____

_____

18. Rank the four most important values in your life in order of importance

_____

_____

_____

_____

_____

19. When your feathers get ruffled, how do you show it?

_____

_____

_____

_____

_____

20. When you need support, how will I know?

_____

_____

_____

_____

_____

21. On what other topics do you feel we need to reach some points of agreement?

_____

_____

_____

_____

_____

Explore New Nest Design

An important key to nesting success is the openness to a new design. You may have been comfortable in your old nest structure even if the nestmate was a real bedbug. But this nest must accommodate an entirely new flock unused to coexisting. A good negotiated design will go a long way toward creating long-term nesting satisfaction.

What do you want this new nest to look and feel like? You need to design the nest in mutual agreement and then contract to be committed to the design. When the hen and rooster are in agreement, you create cohesiveness, credibility and consistency for the entire flock.

How to Use This Worksheet:

After reading and discussing each person's "Nest History" worksheet together, it is time to prepare or repair the nest. Do this with the "Our New Nest Should" worksheet.

Worksheet Purpose:

After reading and discussing the "Nest History" worksheet, you will begin the "Our New Nest Should" worksheet. This worksheet is to aid you in the design of your blended nest. It will help you reach points of agreement as a couple on important issues that affect the success of your family.

Worksheet Directions:

1. Make an appointment for this experience.

2. Sit down together in a relaxing place.

3. This is the first of what may be several sessions.

4. Bring the "Nest History" worksheets with you.

5. Begin carefully working through each question on "Our New Nest Should."

6. Be present in a spirit of negotiation and compromise.

Our New Nest Should

1. The four most important values on which we would like to build our new nest are ...

    _____
    _____
    _____
    _____
    _____

2. Important celebrations in our nest will be ...

    _____
    _____
    _____
    _____
    _____

3. Disciplinary guidelines in our nest are ...

    _____
    _____
    _____
    _____
    _____

4. The way hen/rooster disagreements in our nest will be handled is ...

    _____
    _____
    _____
    _____
    _____

5. The way ex-nestmate relationships will be handled in our nest is ...

    _____
    _____
    _____
    _____
    _____

6. Manners important to the success of our nest are ...

_____

_____

_____

_____

_____

7. The way rules in our nest will be constructed is ...

_____

_____

_____

_____

_____

8. Basic moral values important to our nest are ...

_____

_____

_____

_____

_____

9. Religion in our nest will be ...

_____

_____

_____

_____

_____

10. The three things we want most for our nest are ...

_____

_____

_____

_____

_____

Include Hen and Rooster Bonding Opportunities in the Master Design

A stepmom interviewed for this book put it like this, "We were so busy being a family that we didn't take enough time to nurture our relationship. I think we saw it as an important thing at the time to give all of our time to the kids. When we neglected our couple bonding, I began to feel resentment."

What about a hen/rooster contract that looks like this?

Hen/Rooster Contract

We realize that strong couple cohesiveness is important to the success of this family, therefore:

We will make time to nurture our couple relationship.

We will tell and show our children
that our partner is first in our lives.

We will value each other.

We will value each child.

We will surpass blood kin, exes, extended family
and community, and do what is best for each other
and each child.

Signatures: _____

Date: _____

After the couple has outlined what it feels the new nest should look like, other family members need to be brought into the design process. The how-to's of doing that will be discussed in the next chapter.

Nest-Planning Summary

If you are frightened about the shape of your new nest, don't panic. Any chick or rooster who isn't scared simply doesn't care about succeeding. Write the word S-C-A-R-E-D. Now cross out the S. Then cross out the D. What you have left is the word CARE. We are **scared** to attempt anything we really **care** about. The key is: Don't be too chicken to try!

The best way to succeed is to plan. You have tools to examine how you really feel about the structure of this new nest, for communicating how you really feel about this design.

Many biologically intact families would benefit by doing this same exercise. Chicken-fights result when you have unexpressed expectations and want your nestmate to assimilate these expectations by osmosis.

In Chapter One you began thinking through your hopes for success. Chapter Two will give you tools for realistically examining the flock's expectations and designing a workable nest structure.

Even though the chickenyard may predict your doom, you can choose to flourish. I like the thought that is expressed by Galway Kinnell in this line ... *"Let our scars fall in love."*

> *"A man begins cutting his wisdom teeth the first time he bites off more than he can chew."*
>
> Herb Caen

C HAPTER 2

Determining the Shape of the Nest

"So what are we supposed to call you, anyway?"

"I do not ask of God that he should change anything in events themselves, but that he should change me in regard to things, so that I might have the power to create my own universe..."

Nerval

"We must work at the future as weavers work at high warp tapestry: without seeing it."

Anatole France

What Does a "Normal" Nest Look Like?

No one in any societal group thinks the stepfamily is "normal." Normal means "usual or typical." When we look at the definition of this word and compare it with statistics from the Stepfamily Foundation, we find that stepfamilies *are* the norm of the late 20th century. The Stepfamily Foundation statistics tell us that:

• 50 million Americans are currently in step relationships.

• By the year 2000, there will be more stepfamilies than "original" or nuclear families.

• A half million couples with children remarry every year.

2

So how do you deal with this new status quo? How do you cope with Stepfamily Foundation statistics that tell you things like:

- Children from "intact" homes do better on 14 of 16 classroom behavior ratings.

- They do better in social adjustment (popularity, ability to communicate, getting along with others), and school work (higher IQs, better grades, greater self-discipline).

- Only 45% of children do well after divorce.

- Most children of divorce have acute problems with self-esteem.

Biologically intact families have challenging problems to overcome too, but it's the stepfamilies people choose to focus on for statistics of dysfunctional behavior.

The barnyard critics don't expect the stepfamily to succeed. Comments I became familiar with were, "You'll never make it," "I sure don't envy you," "I'll give it six months," "Remember, you can always get out."

This Is Going to Be a Strange Kind of Nest

I was determined not to listen to any of the sharp beaks in the yard, but my first thought that maybe I *should* have listened actually came on the day before our wedding. The wedding itself should have given me the final proof that our nest was never going to be normal.

Three small bodies were bouncing off the walls of my apartment. Out-of-town cousins were sometimes dodging flying toys and at other times joining in the activities in self-defense and to stave off boredom.

Family and friends were in every corner of the tiny apartment, and there was food on every available surface. Coffee tables had become places to sit and no square inch of usable space was ignored. We were in the middle of rehearsal dinner, and I was coping in this wired chicken coop because of the knowledge that in less

2

than an hour I would be out the door! I was spending the night with my matron of honor to get ready for the wedding in peace and quiet.

I comforted myself with the thought that if we could just get through this night and the next morning, the wedding itself would go smoothly. Hadn't I organized state conventions for hundreds of people that had been praised for their excellence? What were just a hundred or so friends and family in a small church with a cozy ceremony? What could possibly go wrong?

As I entered the sanctuary and made the turn to walk down the aisle, I noticed that several people were snickering. My matron of honor had just thoroughly checked out my appearance and I was confident there were no bra straps showing, no unruly strands of hair, no toilet paper trailing from my shoe.

Just as I was thinking of checking again, I looked down the aisle at my soon-to-be husband. I expected this to be a sacred moment. One where our eyes would meet and lock. One where everyone watching would know how much we were in love and be engulfed in our happiness.

I never got to look in Steve's eyes because his shoes caught my attention, took my breath away and laid waste my fantasies of the perfect wedding. The only thing I could focus on were the Batman tennis shoes that he and his attendants were wearing! As the audience noticed me looking, snickers gave way to guffaws. For some reason, I kept on going down that aisle. I assumed that was the last surprise of the wedding. Big mistake, assuming.

After the minister asked Steve, "Do you take this woman...," before answering, Steve looked at his brother-in-law for confirmation. Pete nodded, "Yes." Steve next looked at each of the three children in turn. Each child nodded, "Yes." He last checked with his best man who gave his assent, then turned to the minister and said, "Yes," himself.

One guest remarked later, "This is the most fun wedding I've ever attended." Another guest commented, "This wedding was anything but normal and boring." The wedding was not smooth, boring or normal. I should have recognized it as great training for the fancy footwork required in the coop.

> *"The poet doesn't invent. He listens."*
>
> Jean Cocteau

2

How Do We Design a Nest That Works for Us?

Anything worthwhile takes time and work. Successful biological flocks do not happen by accident either. The stepfamily can provide a unique way to teach members to deal with change management, creative problem-solving, conflict management and diversity. Each of these issues are life problems that we face in the 21st century coop and yard.

The stepfamily can be an incubator where you learn to be functional in a challenging coop. You can learn to deal with broken shells and ruffled feathers and experience the satisfaction that comes from meeting the challenges of the coop and mastering them.

Research will help your stepfamily confront this different kind of nest. You need to:

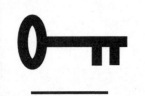

- Look at what you consider to be the ideal nest

- Note how your nest is different

- Decide what you want to call each other (and other members of the yard)

- Share your "nestpectations"

- Find your definition of success

- Provide some examples of success

- Find common ground

This **Successful Nest Ingredients** tool will also help you realize and talk about:

- It's OK that we are different.
- It's OK that we are sometimes happy and sometimes unhappy.
- It's OK that what we want and what we have sometimes do not match.

Worksheet Directions:

1. Each family member fills out the worksheet.

2. Set a time for the worksheet to be completed, and hold a family meeting for discussion and future action.

3. At the time of the family meeting, responses to the first three questions should be shared and discussed.

4. Compare and discuss the family-tree drawings in number four. You could even ask a family artist to draw a composite, and you can post it somewhere.

5. Now that you know what to do with numbers one through four, what to do with numbers five through nine will be explained following the worksheet.

> *"The optimist invented the aeroplane, the pessimist the parachute."*
>
> Anonymous

What Does Our Family Look Like?

"If I could wish for my life to be perfect, it would be tempting but I would decline, for life would no longer teach me anything."

Allyson Jones

1. List five qualities of the ideal nest.

   _____
   _____
   _____
   _____
   _____

2. How is our nest different from this ideal?

   _____
   _____
   _____
   _____
   _____

3. How is our nest like this ideal?

_____
_____
_____
_____
_____

4. Draw a family tree for us. (Use a separate sheet of paper and get help when you need it.)

5. What do we want to call each other?

_____
_____
_____
_____
_____

6. What I expected when I became a part of this nest was ...

_____
_____
_____
_____
_____

7. Our nest will be more successful when ...

_____
_____
_____
_____
_____

"All great discoveries are made by mistake."

Harold Faber

8. One success our nest has already had was ...

_____

_____

_____

_____

_____

9. .I think everyone in our nest could agree on ...

_____

_____

_____

_____

_____

Naming the Members of the Flock

For some reason, many people have the same negative reaction to family titles beginning with "step" that they have to the word "criticism." They feel nothing about a word beginning with "step" can be positive or complimentary. A number of suggestions for substitutions for "step" terminology have been presented, from the sublime to the totally ridiculous.

Consider "a rose by any other name would smell as sweet." A word is only as ugly or bothersome as the intent of the person saying it. When you say, "This is my stepmother/father/child," with pride, honor is attached to the word.

Use terminology which is least confusing to the eggs. Asking an egg to call a stepchick, "Mom" can be very confusing and can cause a great deal of conflict (especially if the egg doesn't want to do it). On the other hand, if the egg says, "Is it OK if I call you Mom?" that's a different issue. The important thing is that you have an open-nest discussion to deal with what is comfortable for each of you.

In my nest the three eggs had always called me "Ruth-Ann" until we saw the movie, "Hook." In that movie, the leader of the lost boys is "Rufeo." The eggs began to call me that (no

2

specific meaning intended), and I found that I really liked it. It has become a real term of endearment and one that is unique to our family.

When introducing each other, we say with pride, "This is my stepson/daughter/mom." The children's biomom is a very active part of their lives and it is confusing to everyone for there to be two "Moms."

You also need to think about how you refer to the biochick or rooster. When you say, "*Your* mom/dad...," understand that *you* in all its forms is a blaming word. Eggs do not need to feel blamed for the behavior of any member of the yard.

The function of the nest is to protect the eggs. Referring to the other chick or rooster by their given name is a protecting behavior. It does not indicate blame. It simply gives reference to a yard member not in this particular nest. So, instead of saying, "*Your* mom/dad ..." or "*Your* stepmom/dad," consider saying, "JoAnne is picking you up at 5:00 p.m. today," or "Bill will spend next weekend with you."

Egg protection can best occur by naming, not blaming.

> *"It is not the mountain we conquer, but ourselves."*
>
> Edmund Hillary

How Do Nestpectations Influence Reality?

"Reality can destroy the dream, why shouldn't the dream destroy reality?"

George Moore

Question number six is important as an attitude barometer. In *Psychology of Winning,* Denis Waitley says, "We become what we expect ourselves to become." What you expect of your nest has a lot to do with what your nest actually becomes. This is a great opportunity to remind each flock member that their expectations affect each chicken and egg individually and the nest as a whole.

What you really get is what you really expect. One of the ways you can best calm flapping wings is to expect no ruffled feathers.

I always dreaded going to events where the biomom would be present. I expected that it would damage the shells of the eggs, cause the rooster to squawk and the chicks to square off.

What actually happened was that the eggs ran themselves ragged trying to hop between nests and not offend either chick, the rooster tried to fade into the chickenyard and this chick couldn't keep down the worms she had just tried to digest. I got exactly what I expected.

I began to accept these yard meetings as inevitable parts of life in the coop. I explained to the eggs that I was not comfortable sitting or standing next to the other chick and that they didn't have to choose between us. The eggs were relieved with the honesty and relieved of the pretense.

When you assume that the eggs are believing false pretenses of "liking" the other chick or rooster, you dirty the coop and erase possibilities of teaching them about honesty in emotions.

> *"Striving is perhaps the one and only true elixir, for while we converse with what is above us, we do not grow old, but grow young."*
>
> Ralph Waldo Emerson

Writing a Contract to Smooth Ruffled Feathers

Question number seven can lead you to an important action. You need to contract with each other for a peaceful flock existence.

From your meeting that came after the worksheet, you should have gained:

- reinforcement that you can be in the nest together without pushing each other out.

- a beginning knowledge of each nest member's nestpectations.

- a start on naming the flock

- each flock member's definition of success

2

You can begin to pull together by adopting a family motto and by focusing on the one point on which you can all agree. The family motto will come as you pull together bits and pieces of each person's answer to question number seven. For example, these could have been some of the answers to question seven:

We can agree that this isn't much fun.
We can agree that we are confused.
We can agree that we'd like to get along better.
We can agree that we need some rules.

This might lead to a family point of agreement which says:

To get along better and to avoid confusion, we need to make some rules together. Maybe we can start by treating each other with kindness.

Now you can leave this meeting with a family contract signed by each of you to respect this point of agreement.

The family contract might look like this:

Family Contract

This point of agreement is our family's cornerstone.
(Write in the point of agreement here.)

_____

_____

_____

We will respect this agreement and value its importance to the growth of each individual and to the peace of our flock.

Signatures: _____

Date: _____

Note: The word "peace" in this contract is better initially than "success." Some flock members may not feel that they want success right now. That peaceful feeling will have to be nourished and allowed to mature. You are just beginning a process of understanding. Even if you have been in your stepfamily for a long time, you are starting over.

This contract should be laminated and/or framed and placed in a position of importance and easy reference.

When conflict arises, the flock can first turn to the contract, remember the point of agreement and begin conflict negotiation in a positive way.

Nest-Design Summary

Your nest will be most stress free when you design it together.

Nestpectations of each egg, chick and rooster need to be examined.

Clear communication about these nestpectations will enhance your chances for successful coop existence.

"The tighter the construction, the easier the cleaning is and the fewer cracks and crevices there will be where pathogens and parasites can hide."

from *The Chicken Health Handbook*

> *"Don't take action because of a name! A name is an uncertain thing,; you can't count on it!"*
>
> Bertolt Brecht

> *"Names are but noise and smoke, obscuring heavenly light."*
>
> Goethe

2

C HAPTER 3

Prevent Disease from Surviving in Your Yard

"I think we have the step-pox!"

The most infectious disease that can enter your chickenyard is distemper. The disease manifests itself in statements like, "Love her? I don't even like her! How can you ask me to love her?" The distemper runs through the flock infecting even those eggs, chicks and roosters who originally had good intentions toward their nestmates.

If one member of the nest begins to display the following symptoms, it won't be long before the distemper spreads to another and another, until the nest becomes a place of utter silence or constant pushing and shoving for position:

1. Withdrawal from the flock

2. Negative clucking

3. Collecting mud

> *"It takes longer for man to find out man than any other creature that is made."*
>
> Henry Ward Beecher

3

Distemper Begins in Lack of Understanding

On November 25, 1989, I walked down that church aisle and became a stepparent. On November 26, 1989, I listened to Cam and Steve arguing in the living room. I watched Stephanie and Ross standing in the bedroom door eyeing me with confusion as they came to say good morning to their dad and found me in his bed. I could readily identify with Chicken Little's famous cry, "The sky is falling." I saw myself as a hen sitting on a nest that was infiltrated with beings I didn't understand. My peace and quiet shattered forever, I looked for ways to bring some order into the chicken yard.

By the grace of God, through trial and error and with tears and hugs, we discovered together that we could beat the negatives. We could move from being a group of people who felt forced into contact to a group who really love and respect each other.

You probably know some stepfamilies who never get to the point where they can honestly make a declaration of love for each other. Some are doing well if they can just get to "I like you." And some will consider "I have agreed to tolerate you" as progress.

Beat Disease with Understanding

Understanding means:

- To know (What do other members of the nest like to do?)

- To be tolerant of (Think more of what you like about the flock than what you dislike.)

- To be sympathetic toward (Realize that each bird is trying to find his position in the nest.)

In a stepfamily you can actually even "be empathetic toward." You are all in this chickenhouse together. You can understand that one of the things you each have in common is insecurity.

There are three levels of understanding that the stepfamily needs to work to achieve. They are:

UNDERSTANDING *(head knowledge)* "I know..."
I can "know," have head knowledge of you.
For example, "I know you enjoy playing baseball."

UnderSTANDING *(heart knowledge)* "I feel..."
I can "feel" with you, and this time my heart gets into the act. "I feel sorry that you had to move into my nest. I know this must make you feel sad."

UNDERstanding *(hands-on knowledge)* "I support..."
When I know you and feel with you, I show this by supporting you. I get hands-on involved in trying to help you. I may help you study for a test or attend a contest you're participating in.

Each level of understanding takes us one step closer to a family member. It is really tough to resent someone you understand in these three ways.

How can we work on this understanding in our nest? What tools are found in the barnyard?

"The deep sea can be fathomed, but who knows the hearts of men?"

Malay Proverb

Worksheet Directions:

1. Explain the different meanings of understanding to the family group or to each individual before beginning the worksheet.

2. Before beginning, know your audience.

   A. What family members will be eager to cooperate?

   B. What family members may refuse to cooperate?

3. To get more family members on board, tell them what they have to gain by cooperating.

   Examples: "When you do this exercise, it will be easier to get your stepbrother to help you clean your room."

3

> *"Them which is of other natures thinks different."*
>
> Charles Dickens

"When you do this exercise, it will be easier to persuade your dad to attend your ball game."

4. Know that even if you do this exercise alone, it will help you know how to initiate cooperation and understanding between and among other family members.

5. This exercise may be done:

   • alone

   • in a complete family group meeting

   • in a partial family group meeting

6. After completing the exercise, set your individual goals for increased understanding of each family member.

Understanding My Nest Members

1. What do I know about the other members of my stepfamily?

   List the name of each member of your stepfamily and one fact you know about that person.

   _____   _____
   _____   _____
   _____   _____
   _____   _____
   _____   _____
   _____   _____

2. What do I feel about the other members of my stepfamily?

   List the name of each member of your stepfamily and list one good feeling you have about each person.

   _____   _____
   _____   _____
   _____   _____
   _____   _____
   _____   _____
   _____   _____

3. In what ways do I support the other members of my stepfamily?

   a. What does support mean to me?

   b. What do I think support means to the other members of my family?

   _____   _____
   _____   _____
   _____   _____
   _____   _____
   _____   _____
   _____   _____

4. My goal is to support one family member next week.

   I choose to support _____.

   I am supporting _____because _____ _____ _____

   The way I will support _____ is _____ _____ _____

"There are no elements so diverse that they cannot be joined in the heart of a man."

Jean Giraudoux

3

> *"There never were, in the world, two opinions alike, no more than two hairs, or two grains; the most universal quality is diversity."*
>
> Montaigne

Some Understanding Thoughts from the Larger Yard to Guide You

"Understanding is the beginning of approval."

Andre Gide

"To understand is to forgive, even oneself."

Alexander Chase

"One learns people through the heart, not the eyes or the intellect."

Mark Twain

How to Survive in the Nest Without Love

OK, so you didn't fall instantly in love with your stepchildren. The love that our family has come to was not an overnight process. We have been working hard for six years, not always together, to be able to sincerely say to each other, "I love you."

Not all chickens or eggs experience love at first sight — in fact, most don't. How do you find warmth in a strange nest when you honestly can't say you love the other birds? How can you tolerate these avian imposters without pecking at each other when you don't even really like them?

You may not be able to love instantly. What you can do is be kind to the rest of the brood. What is the difference between love and kindness?

Love: an intense, affectionate concern for another person

Kindness: showing evidence of sympathy or concern for others

Kindness is not so tough. You are kind to people who need help in grocery stores, on street corners, in elevators, at school,

3

at work and at church. You are kind to perfect strangers. Why is it so tough to be kind to those living in your own chicken coop?

It's harder to be kind to those in the coop because you have to live with them daily. The feeding habits, manners and attitudes that other members of the brood have learned over a lifetime are comfortable for you. Your lip-smacking as you eat has never bothered you, but it drives me crazy! You may not want to change, and change will be hard or perhaps even uncomfortable for you.

There are several steps in hatching the art of kindness. These kindness steps are in order of maturation. One step must be mastered to move to the next.

> *"Minds are like parachutes. They only function when they are open."*
>
> Sir James Dewar

The Steps in Hatching Kindness

1. Make a hole in your resistance shell by respecting the habits of different breeds.

   Easy to say, harder to do. Each of the birds in this nest has been raised with different feeding habits, cleaning habits and communication habits.

   You need to respect those differences. You can never negotiate for change until you understand that those differences are learned behaviors for each person in our family. Winston Churchill said, *"Personally I'm always ready to learn, although I do not always like being taught."*

   Few breeds change their habits without a chicken-fight. Who's going to decide which habits of which breed are "right" and which are "wrong?" Carl Rogers said, *"The curious paradox is that when I accept myself just as I am, then I can change."* The first step in hatching is to accept the other chickens and eggs just as they are.

2. Take the top off the shell and look around for ways to be kind.
   A. Be courteous
   B. Be pleasant
   C. Be helpful
   D. Be friendly

3

E. Be generous

F. Be a cheerleader

In order to be courteous, pleasant, helpful, friendly, generous or to cheerlead, you must know how each bird defines each of these words.

3. Break out of the shell to share the suffering of the flock.

A. What kinds of suffering do flock members sometimes experience?

B. How could you share this suffering?

How to Use the Hatching Steps

1. Read through these steps individually or in a nest meeting. (A good way to begin this meeting would be to discuss the idea of "random acts of kindness." Share stories about a time when someone was kind to you for no reason.)

2. Prepare a group list of reactions to what each of the words in step two mean and what acts would show these feelings.

3. Post a list of "acts of kindness" which can serve as a reminder.

4. Have each flock member prepare a "kindnesses" jar with his name on it. In this jar, he will have placed strips of paper with ideas for ways others could be kind to him.

5. Decide what the flock will do to celebrate or how to say thank you when another member of the brood has been kind.

Three Steps Our Family Has Taken to Nourish Our Newly Hatched Kindness

3

These are steps you can take to begin to understand other coopmates. Use them to help your new brood mature into a cohesive flock.

1. Partner the brood to solve problems.

A. Each person has a right to speak and express feelings.

B. As you express feelings, you also offer solutions that you're comfortable with and think will work.

C. You then take a piece of each person's solution and weave those pieces together for a creative solution to your problem.

D. Because each of you had a part in the solution, you own this solution and are more likely to comply with it.

> *"Kindness is the golden chain by which society is bound together."*
>
> Goethe

We put these same ideas to work at home to solve a baby-sitting problem. When Cameron was almost thirteen, we once hired a fourteen-year-old to "big-kid sit" (there had been a negative kid backlash to the term "baby-sitting"). As we left, Steve and I began to see that the small age difference was pretty ludicrous. We devised a system to have each kid sit himself.

Here's how we made it work. Before we leave, each child makes a list of "rules" for himself. We then all go to the computer and get a list of rules for everyone. Each child is responsible for his own behavior while we are gone. When we return, if there is no blood and the house is still standing, each kid gets paid for being responsible for himself. This has been a very workable system for us.

In families where each member feels ownership of the "nest," there is less squawking and greater understanding of nest rules. Your eggs will think they have a right to live in a place that they helped to plan. Incorporate their ideas into almost every decision you make.

3

> *"Kindness gives birth to kindness."*
>
> Sophocles

2. Scratching out feelings is easier at first.

When your brood is not even certain they like each other, it's hard to talk and express feelings honestly. You don't even know each other very well, and self-disclosure is tough for eggs even when they come from the same chick and rooster.

Writing feelings on paper seems to depersonalize those feelings and make it easier to openly express feelings.

We began our nest turnaround with something called "The Stepegg Survey." I was desperate for ways for us to relate to each other. I wanted to know what they wanted me to look like in my stepmom role. I decided the best way to get an answer was to ask a question, and so I developed the following survey. Use it to help your eggs.

The Stepegg Survey

1. If you could give advice to a stepparent, what are the three most important things you would tell him?

   _____

   _____

   _____

   _____

   _____

2. What advice would you give a kid who is getting a new stepparent?

   _____

   _____

   _____

   _____

   _____

3. What actions can a stepparent and stepkid take to get along better with each other?

_____

_____

_____

_____

_____

4. What's the best time you've ever had with your stepparent?

_____

_____

_____

_____

_____

5. Do you like for your stepparent to go to parent-teacher conferences?

_____

_____

_____

_____

_____

6. Do you like it when your stepparent attends your athletic games, plays and music and drama programs?

_____

_____

_____

_____

_____

7. What can you do to help your stepparent like you?

_____

_____

_____

_____

_____

> *"A little more than kin, and less than kind."*
>
> Shakespeare

3

8. What can your stepparent do to help you like them?

_____

_____

_____

_____

_____

After the children complete this survey, you'll be amazed at what you learned about them. The learning will be very positive, and the eggs will be really glad to have a chance to express themselves.

One of the things Cameron said in answer to number one (about advice to a new stepparent) was, "I would tell them that as soon as the kids come over, to talk the rules out. To let them say where they want to play or to work. And to let them get used to the house with a new person." Stephanie's answers to number two (advice to a kid getting a new stepparent) were, "I have one too. Treat them nice. Don't worry."

Prevent Disease Summary

One of the toughest diseases for a flock to beat is lack of caring, which leads to resentment. In this chapter you've learned some ways to express kindness. This expression of kindness to the other birds nourishes the developing eggs and reduces stress for the chick and rooster. In the next chapter, you'll find ways to reduce the anger and resentment that create harmful chick-fighting in the nest.

Even if you never feel that you can say, "I love this egg," you can say, "I care about the welfare of this egg." It's virtually impossible to dislike a member of the brood when you're working on being kind to that person.

As our family practiced the ideas in this chapter, we felt that even if the sky does seem to be falling once in a while, we now have some ideas about how to put the pieces back.

> *"All persons are puzzles until at last we find*
> *in some word or act the key to the man, to the woman."*
>
> Emerson

"There is no beautifier of complexion, or form, or behavior, like the wish to scatter joy and not pain around us."

Emerson

CHAPTER 4

Who Are These Eggs, and What Are They Doing in My Nest?

"Let's see, what do we have here?"

"Who has not sat before his own heart's curtain?
It lifts: and the scenery is falling apart."

Rainer Maria Rilke

The State of the Chickenyard

Stepchick/Steprooster:
"It's Thursday night. Friday afternoon those rotten eggs will be coming for the weekend."

Eggs:
"Oh no! It's Thursday. Tomorrow I've got to go spend the whole weekend with that constantly clucking stepchick."

                           or

"Oh no! It's Thursday. Tomorrow I've got to go spend the whole weekend with that touchy steprooster."

As chickens and eggs think about spending the weekend together, you begin to examine your feelings.

> *"It takes an average person almost twice as long to understand a sentence that uses a negative approach than it does to understand a positive sentence."*
>
> John H. Reitmann

> *"The next message you need is always right where you are."*
>
> Ram Dass

As stepchick or steprooster you:

a. Feel resentment. Plan to clean your closet and/or watch TV with the bedroom door locked. They don't want you around anyway.

b. Experience frustration. Pray for a business appointment which will give you a legitimate excuse to be gone until after the eggs are laid in bed. This ensures that the irresponsible chicken who got you into this mess will be stuck with egg sitting all by herself. Maybe she will develop greater appreciation for the cozy nest times with just the two of you nested in!

c. Hope for the best. Suck in your breath. Ask that other chicken to help you plan an activity that has appeal for each nest member and that the flock can do together (if she isn't too chicken). Focus positive thoughts on how this activity will be enjoyed by each member of the flock, will benefit each chicken or egg and will help you be closer in the nest.

As biochick or biorooster you:

a. Feel resentment. Wonder how long it will take that chicken you live with to prove that she is chicken this time? That locking herself in her part of the nest is really too much! Ask yourself why she hates the eggs so much. What have they ever done to her?

b. Experience frustration. Wonder how creative the business excuse will be this time to keep her "at work" long after the kids are in bed. Feel tired and lonely thinking about dealing with the kids alone. Wish for a "normal" family feeling.

c. Hope for the best. Suck in your breath. Ask your spouse to help you plan an activity that has appeal for each family member and that can be done together. Focus positive thoughts on how this activity will be enjoyed by each person, will benefit each person and will bring you together as a family.

As the egg you...

a. Feel resentment. Wonder why my stepchick/rooster doesn't like us. She never wants to do any activities with us. Wonder if she will be leaving us soon.

b. Feel relief. She always finds something to do when we come so that she doesn't have to spend time with us. It does make it easier just to spend time with my real chick/rooster.

c. Hope for the best. Maybe this time we can plan an activity that we can all enjoy and do together. I think I'd like to get to know this chicken better.

> *"No man is angry that feels not himself hurt."*
>
> Francis Bacon

As each of you worked through these answers, you found one that best described your feelings.

If A fit you best: You are at the beginning stage in the nest. You need to admit your resentment and get it out of the way so you can move past it and grow to be a healthy group.

If B fit you best: You are at the avoidance stage in the nest. You need to learn to hop out of that comfortable corner of the nest you've been hiding in and face each other honestly.

If C fit you best: You are making progress in the nest. You are ready to venture into this chickenyard without pecking and squawking.

> *"When angry,*
> *count four. When*
> *very angry, swear."*
>
> Mark Twain

How Can We Get This Aviary to Be Less Alien?

Do you ever feel that you're in Never-Never Land? You're always pretending, always expected to be someone you don't know how to be and always expected to feel things you're not really feeling. Honesty about feelings can allow us to use this "stuff" we're constantly stepping in as fertilizer!

When I was able to admit to myself, "I'm not really crazy about this nest or this flock," I was able to begin getting rid of my resentment and start building a better nest. When I began to start building, I realized that the eggs needed the same opportunity and I looked for ways to help us get more comfortable with each nestmate.

Stepchicks and roosters need to be free to ask, "Who are these eggs, and what are they doing in my nest?" Stepeggs need to be free to peck along at, "How did I get stuck in this alien aviary?"

Admit How You Really Feel in This Henhouse

In order not to feel alone in this strange place, in order to stop spending time sitting in the middle of the chickenhouse crying, "I don't belong," you need a plan. You need the freedom and the courage to say to yourself what you really feel. You need to be honest about how you feel so you can admit it and grow past it.

So, the first step is, "Admit what you really feel!"

I am a "what you see is what you get" sort of chick. I was being pressured by the entire yard (with special pressure from the rooster) to immediately say that I loved these eggs. I was pressured by the biomom to like and to communicate with her. I felt socially unacceptable to almost everyone when I couldn't honestly do any of the above.

When the yard would ask me, "How's it going?" I would force a smile and say (through clenched beak), "Great!" I was lying through that beak, and I've never been comfortable with lying. I felt that I was living a lie to myself and the entire flock.

The Honest Chicken Checkup

Check any of the next statements you have ever wanted the courage/permission to just crow from the top of the chickenhouse.

- ☐ "This is not fun."
- ☐ "This "stuff" is awful."
- ☐ "Nobody in this yard likes me."
- ☐ "I'm not really crazy about these eggs."
- ☐ "Everyone here wishes I were in another nest."
- ☐ "Why did I get myself into this nest?"
- ☐ "What a mess!"
- ☐ "Get me out of here!"
- ☐ "Will that biochick/rooster just strut on down the road and get a life in her own nest so things can go well in ours (and by the way, I really dislike her)?"
- ☐ "Why, every time things are going just great, does the biochick/rooster drop a load of fertilizer in the middle of this nest?"
- ☐ "Where's the farmer so I can complain about conditions in this yard?"
- ☐ "Why do I have to be the first chick/rooster to stop pecking and start chirping?"

> *"A man that does not know how to be angry does not know how to be good."*
>
> Henry Ward Beecher

The Advantages of Unpretentious Pecking

What good will admitting your feelings do? James Pennebaker says in *Opening Up: The Healing Power of Confiding in Others*:

"Not disclosing our thoughts and feelings can be unhealthy. Divulging them can be healthy."

" ... admitting our emotions to ourselves and others serves an important communicative function."

" ... By talking about upsetting events, people achieve insight into the events and learn more about themselves. With this knowledge, people can put the traumas behind them."

4

> *"Let not the sun go down upon your wrath."*
>
> Ephesians 4:26

How to Use the Plain-Pecking Worksheet:

The idea that nest members have to pretend, fake or be dishonest with the nest and yard is an unhealthy one. You need a legitimate way to be honest but not brutal about your feelings. You need to talk about your upsets, resentments and anger to get these traumas out of the yard and open up growth opportunities in your nest.

You need to be able to express to someone how you truly feel so that you can get past these feelings and mature. First you have to be honest with yourself. This exercise can help you be more honest.

David Augsberger said, *"... I am discovering that anger that is expressed in assertive and affirmative ways can be powerful and healing."*

Worksheet Directions:

1. Do this worksheet individually and in separate areas of the nest. Do numbers one through three individually. Number four will be done as a flock.

2. Take your time with this worksheet. It may be one that takes a week to think about, gather ideas and gather courage to express real feelings.

3. Together, set a time for all flock members to be finished with the worksheet.

4. Collect the worksheets on the deadline.

5. Each flock member will have a set time to take all of the worksheets and read them.

6. After each nester has read the worksheets, have a nest meeting to discuss how to approach setting the goal(s) in number four.

7. Post the goal(s) in number four in the common area, where nesters can remind themselves of the goal.

The Plain-Pecking Worksheet

a. I sometimes feel resentment because ...

_____

_____

_____

_____

_____

b. I think other members of my nest feel resentment because ...

_____

_____

_____

_____

_____

c. In the past, I have dealt with my resentment by ...

_____

_____

_____

_____

_____

d. The way I want to deal with resentment in the future is ...

_____

_____

_____

_____

_____

"I know of no more disagreeable situation than to be left feeling generally angry without anybody in particular to be angry at."

Frank Moore Colby

4

This exercise helps each nester to know and understand her own resentment. It also helps the flock know that others are also feeling some disenchantment with the nesters and the nest arrangements. This can actually bring forward some pecking issues.

Let's Vent Some Common Pecking Issues

4

Here are some of the things I found I resented.

• I resented the biochick because she was a part of the life of the eggs and the rooster before I was.

• I resented the continuing ties to the biochick for the eggs and my rooster.

• I resented not being the biochick of these eggs.

• I resented the expectations of the biochick on my time and money.

• I resented the expectations of the biochick on my rooster. (Even "please have him call" can be irritating!)

The list was long. Once I had written it down, I felt spent and satisfied. These were real feelings and I needed to see them. Each nest has different problems that cause resentment, and many of you have problems in common. What about these pecking problems?

• Divorce decrees that read like marriage contracts

• Needy chickens who don't really want to let go

• Chickens who want even dysfunctional contact

• Chickens who enjoy the control they can still exercise because of the eggs

• Chickens who use eggs as missiles in a Halloween prank

• Chickens who use eggs as carrier pigeons between yards

• Chickens who enjoy interrupting the schedule of your nest and do it on purpose

> *"Many people lose their tempers merely from seeing you keep yours."*
>
> Frank Moore Colby

- Chickens who use you as an unpaid nestsitter

- Chickens who enjoy making other chickens look like fertilizer

- Chickens who drop "stuff" on your head when the nest is cozy

- Biochickens who want a relationship with the new chicken

"Anger is one of the sinews of the soul; he that lacks it hath a maimed mind."

Thomas Fuller

4

The list goes on and on, doesn't it? How do you get past these feelings after admitting them? Recognizing that you're about to step in that "stuff" on the floor of the chickenhouse lets you make a decision to: avoid it, scoop it, sweep it out the door or march on through. What is the content of this "stuff" you find yourself in quite often, and why do you let so much of it collect before you do something about it?

Own Your "Stuff"

Stepping in "stuff" creates anger. But anger is a decision process, not a gut response. You choose to toss your feathers or not to toss them. Tell yourself, "This is my choice. This is my behavior. I can't change anyone but myself. I can choose not to be angry."

You can prepare to make the better choice when you:

A. Know what makes up your "stuff."

My "Stuff" Profile

1. What are some of the things you get angry about in your nest?

_____

_____

_____

_____

_____

4

2. Which eggs/chickens in your nest make you the angriest?

_____
_____
_____
_____
_____

3. What are some of your body reactions when you get angry?

_____
_____
_____
_____
_____

4. What triggers your anger?

_____
_____
_____
_____
_____

> *"Usually when people are sad, they don't do anything. But when they get angry, they bring about a change."*
>
> Malcolm X

B. Prepare for your "stuff."

Say, "I know this is going to make me angry. I can unruffle my own feathers. I can work out a way to handle this. Even in this tough 'stuff,' I believe in myself and my ability to choose my own response. I refuse to step in this 'stuff.' I have other options."

Remember these words of advice as you consider that "to be or not to be" angry and resentful is a conscious choice.

> *"I was angry with my friend:*
> *I told my wrath, my wrath did end.*
> *I was angry with my foe:*
> *I told it not, my wrath did grow."*

C. Gauge how angry you really are.

- Is this a "My feathers are ruffled" or an "I'm running around like a chicken with my head cut off!" situation?

- Ask yourself:
  How much "stuff" is involved in this mess?

- Am I angry about this nest issue, or are there several others that I'm still angry about that are making this one seem worse?

- Are there other flock members who have an interest in seeing this chicken-fight and are "egging" it on?

D. Decide why you're angry.

What feelings or situations are causing this reaction? Do you feel:

☐ threatened?
☐ annoyed?
☐ insulted?
☐ frustrated?
☐ that some chicken/egg is treating you unjustly?
☐ that some chicken/egg has made an unfair demand?

> *"Nothing on earth consumes a man more quickly than the passion of resentment."*
>
> Nietzsche

4

"To state the facts frankly is not to despair for the future, not indict the past."

John F. Kennedy

Choose Your Response to This Nest Mess

As a responsible, problem-solving chicken, you have options. You can choose your response. You won't choose the same response to each yard problem. Here is a partial list of possible responses. You can:

1. Avoid being a paranoid flock member. (Don't assume that "Those other chickens/eggs are out to get me.")

2. Make "stuff" into fertilizer.

3. Don't run around like a chicken with your head cut off or a scrambled egg. Tell yourself, "I'm not going to let this yard get to me."

4. Tell yourself, "I'll just roost and let that chick make a rotten egg of herself. The rest of the yard will notice."

5. Know that your anger is a signal that you need to sort through your "stuff."

6. Ask, "What if we're both flying in the right direction?"

7. Consider forgiving the offending flock member.

8. Ask yourself, "If I get angry, how many minutes of my life am I losing to a stress response? Is this chicken/nest worth actual minutes of my life?" Remember Frederick Buechner's words...

"Of the Seven Deadly Sins, anger is possibly the most fun. To lick your wounds, to smack your lips over grievances long past, to roll over your tongue the prospect of bitter confrontations still to come, to savor to the last toothsome morsel both the pain you are given and the pain you are giving back — in many ways it is a feast fit for a king. The chief drawback is that what you are wolfing down is yourself. The skeleton at the feast is you."

Teach and Learn Assertive Nest Responses

Unexpressed anger leads to resentment. Think about it. You get up in the morning and head for the yard. The outdoors should be a pleasant place to crow and strut. But NO! You begin to think about the flock member or biochick or rooster whom you can't stand! You spend so much time obsessing over this chicken that you totally ruin your wake-up time and get out into the yard looking for a chicken to peck!

You think about this chicken all day and find yourself so angry that you're pushing and shoving in the nest. How much corn could you have gathered had you spent your mental time better?

In the book *Unexpected Answers*, you read, *"Resentment gives someone else space in your mind rent free."* You need all your mental space, don't you? You need to express your anger and free your mind.

When you express your anger, you want to do it in a way that leaves no bodies in its wake. You don't want to be victimized, and you don't want to victimize any other members of the yard.

The behavior categories that can exist in nests are these :

Passive:	The chicken who ***chooses to be a victim***. The "Chicken Little."
Scenario:	It's Sunday night. Garbage collection is on Monday. The garbage is still sitting at the door of the coop rather than at the yard gate where it's supposed to be. A nest member says, "Hey! Whose turn is it to take out the garbage? It's almost midnight, and it's still sitting here in the coop?"
	The *passive* nest member will say, "I know it's not my turn to take out the garbage, but since no one else has done it, I'll do it even though it's not my turn."

> *"To make your children capable of honesty is the beginning of education."*
>
> John Ruskin

> *"No legacy is so rich as honesty."*
>
> Shakespeare

Aggressive: This chicken *creates victims*. Pecks others to hurt them!

The *aggressive* nest member will take this approach to the garbage problem: "I don't know whose turn it is, but I'm not taking it out. I've done it more than I should have already."

Assertive: The assertive nester has *no victims*. This chicken doesn't choose to be pecked by others and doesn't choose to peck others.

The *assertive* nest member will have this solution to the garbage issue: "I know we had a list that rotated the garbage duty. Since we can't seem to find it, let's just make another one and start over tonight."

Passive Aggressive: The passive aggressive nester is the most miserable of all nest members. This chicken *chooses to be a victim and creates victims*.

The *passive aggressive* nest member will do this with the garbage issue:

Volunteer to empty it once again, even though it's another's turn and make certain to spill garbage on the coop floor all the way out of the coop. This nester may even leave a little surprise for the rest of the yard by spreading some garbage in the yard. (This chicken will set her alarm just to be certain she gets to see the unsuspecting yard members step in the garbage as they strut out to crow and stretch their wings the next morning.)

How does each of these barnyard types learn to be assertive and decrease the harmful pecking? Chickens can learn constructive yard behavior.

The Constructive Clucking Conversation

Try this three-step conversation:

1. Describe your feelings fully.

   "I feel ... "

2. Give good reasons for your feelings.

   "Here's why ... "

3. Suggest the behavior you think is fair.

   "Here's what I think is fair ... "
           or
   "In the future, please ... "

Practice this conversation for yourself.

Think of the nestmate to whom you most need to express your anger and resentment. Write your script (the conversation you need to have with this chicken).

The Constructive Clucking Worksheet

1. "I feel ...

   _____
   _____
   _____
   _____
   _____ ."

2. "Here's why ...

   _____
   _____
   _____
   _____
   _____ ."

> *"I hope I shall always possess firmness and virtue enough to maintain what I consider the most enviable of all titles, the character of an 'Honest Man.'"*
>
> George Washington

4

4

3. "Here's what I think is fair ..." OR "In the future, please ...

_____

_____

_____

_____

_____ ."

    Scratching out this clucking plan in advance produces several advantages for each member of the yard.

- You have a chance to see if you really have all the parts ready. (Do you really know what you want, or are you just squawking?)

- By scripting, you've already vented your anger and resentment and begin to unruffle your feathers.

- Seeing this scratched on paper lets you scratch your comb over whether you really need to cluck about it.

- Scripting gives you confidence. If you decide that you really need to have this conversation, you can practice in advance, think of responses the other nester may make and gather courage to go ahead.

- Scripting prevents unloading on your nestmate. You may feel so good about finally having the courage to vent your anger, resentment and frustration that you may unload all of the things that have been building up in your mind for the last six months. Scratching out the script helps you limit yourself to one understandable issue.

> *"Honesty is the single most important factor having a direct bearing on the final success of an individual, corporation or product."*
>
> Ed McMahon

Reap the Rewards of Openness

> *"Truth, like time, is an idea arising from, and dependent upon, human intercourse."*
>
> Isak Dinesen

4

The more flock members feel free to express themselves, the greater respect and kindness you'll experience in the nest. When the nesters feel an environment of secrets and mystery, they become a paranoid flock.

The eggs are the ones most often left to wonder what the chickens have planned next. They hear quietly chirped conversations at night, know that clucking sometimes stops when they enter a corner of the yard and wonder what awful, unexpected piece of sky will fall on them next.

Eggs feel more secure in a yard where they are allowed to participate as full members. When they have no reason to suspect unpleasant surprises, they are free to hatch healthfully.

Our family has grown from a resentful, silent, "Don't touch me" nest to a loud, noisy, "Hey, you forgot to hug me!" flock. We found that constructive clucking produced two great rewards.

1. Constructive clucking increases.
2. Destructive pecking decreases.

How Do These Ideas Work in the Real Yard? Give Us Some Proof.

This chick realized slowly how resentment was affecting her. It took some time of blaming the rest of the yard before I understood that the yard had accepted me, and now I had some work to do on my own. "The Story of the Resentful Chick" will help you understand how things can change in your own heart if you work through these steps. Remember: You can't change anyone but yourself.

The Story of the Resentful Chick

The score was three to two (not in our favor). It was the bottom of the last inning of play in the Kansas City 3-2 Baseball League, Midget B Division, City Championship game. Our team was sitting on TWO outs. My husband Steve was out of town,

4

and I was in charge of my stepson Cameron. In Steve's eyes, I was responsible for Cameron's success. Cameron hadn't played the whole game. I sat miserably on the bench feeling like a failure.

As the clock ticked out the last seconds of this fateful inning, Cameron's coach stepped up to the scorekeeper and said, "Substitute hitter coming in. The name is C-L-U-R-M-A-N." My heart stopped. Why now? Was this coach deliberately sacrificing this kid? Why, with two outs, in the last inning of play, in the city championship game, pick on a kid who hasn't played the whole game? Why put all the eggs in one basket? What horrible pressure for an eleven-year-old.

Cam had been sitting the bench a lot this year. As a young player the first year in a new division, he hadn't had many chances to play. This had been hard on him, but we had worked on sportsmanship and team support. We talked about the fact that from a bench position there was a good deal of time to study the opposition. We isolated the fielding weaknesses of each team. As we talked about the teams, we discovered that the fielding weakness most teams in this division had in common was low, between second and third. That gave us another idea.

We would be prepared so that when Cam did get up to bat, he would make it count. We began working on mental rehearsal, concentrating on visualization exercises. Because the fielding weakness was low, between second and third, we picked an advertising sign in that spot on each field. After other players left at the end of the game, Cam would stand at the plate and swing, visualizing the ball hitting exactly that sign.

Why today for a test of faith? I believed in Cam and I believed in our methods ... BUT ... my gosh!

Cam stepped into the box with a swagger and a confidence I knew he didn't feel. The first pitch came ... he swung ... he missed. I was sweating in mild, 70-degree weather. As the dust from the field turned to mud on my body, I dug my fingers into the arm of the mom sitting next to me. Cam was looking at the next pitch. He swung, he missed.

Every parent on our team was praying, crossing fingers and sitting or standing on the edge of the bleachers. The third pitch came. Cam swung.

The sound of ball against bat was a shout of triumph! Line drive between second and third just the way he had mentally rehearsed. Two batters came home. I cried unashamedly as Cam

> *"You can handle people more successfully by enlisting their feelings than by convincing their reason."*
>
> Paul P. Parker

gave me "thumbs up" with both feet firmly planted on first. The stands went wild! We were hugging people we barely knew. We had won the city championship, and my stepson was a hero.

The next batter drove Cam on home. Cam came past the fence and I was on my feet. As if by rehearsal, our hands were on the fence touching, our smiles were broader than the Missouri River. I felt a wonderful bonding between me and my eldest stepson. I felt like a "real" parent!

On the way out of the stadium, Cam received so many pats on the back and so many words of congratulation that I thought his head would burst. But what meant the most were his words as he put his arm around me, "I'm glad you were here. You're my good-luck charm."

That bonding moment came after a year of being stubbornly uninvolved and resentful. This was Cam's second year in Little League and the first that I made almost every game. The previous year I had been following my resentment policy. I wanted Cam and his dad to have bonding time, but I hated Steve being gone, spending so much time with Cam that should have been MY time. For weeks I stewed, pouted and fumed.

> *"It isn't what happens, it's how you deal with it."*
>
> Anonymous

I also just hated "wasting time out there on those benches." I felt that reading, cleaning house, spending time with my friends, almost anything was better than sitting on those hard bleachers being ignored, watching kids learn to play ball.

Steve repeatedly asked me to attend. Cam said he wanted me to be there. But I was always worried I might encounter "the other chick." I didn't like her. We were worlds apart in almost every way, and yet I was expected to pretend that I knew and liked her. How dishonest!

Finally I got tired of being alone, tired of being left out, tired of not belonging. I resented showing up at games and having to be introduced when other parents were experiencing a real camaraderie. I decided to become an active part of the yard.

I was definitely a part of the yard when paying for clothes, food, the mortgage, kid furniture, movies, toys and entertainment. I was definitely a part of the yard in the time I spent doing laundry, cleaning house and chauffeuring. I was definitely hurting because I was left out. I was confused when, in the other chick's presence, the kids ignored me. I was a "paying" member of this yard in time, money and feelings, and I decided that if I was going to pay, I was going to play!

4

So, this chick made a big discovery. Life in the nest is easier if you participate. The chickenyard functions more effectively if you plan and succeed rather than pout and fail.

Can We Use These Ideas Outside of the Nest?

Some additional applications of the ideas in this chapter outside the immediate nest are:

- Use constructive clucking to deal with the biochick/rooster.
- Use constructive clucking to deal with the extended yard.

Who Are These Eggs Summary

"The old order changeth, yielding place to new."

Tennyson

In order to be a member of my nest in good standing, I finally realized I had to sort out, be honest about and begin to change some of the things I was feeling.

In order to not be alone in the nest, in order to stop spending time sitting in the middle of the nest crying, "I don't belong," I needed a plan. I needed the freedom and the courage to say to myself what I really felt. I needed to be honest about how I felt so that I could admit it and get past it. I needed a way to begin constructive clucking.

That's when I began to use the steps I have shared with you in this chapter.

Virginia Satir says, *"Changing is a matter of becoming honest with your feelings. Being emotionally honest is the heart of making contact. I call this condition of being emotionally honest congruence. The sad thing is that most people take emotional dishonesty for granted and are unaware that anything else is possible. When people do not feel congruent, their relationships become a series of power plays and win/lose operations, thus making little opportunity for them to have good relationships with each other."*

The steps in this chapter will help you work toward emotional honesty in your nest. When you begin being honest, you'll notice many positive changes in your nest. When you begin being honest, you'll be strong enough to conquer the parasites that love to prey on your flock. You'll begin to be a nest that works together for each member of the flock to be successful.

Remember that anger itself is not bad. It's the improper use of anger to destroy the nest that is harmful. Anger is also harmful when individual members of the nest harm themselves by holding feelings inside that need to be dealt with internally or expressed externally and worked through in the nest.

Aristotle helps us understand when he says in the *Nicomachean Ethics*:

> *"Anyone can become angry — that is easy,*
> *but to be angry ...*
> *with the right person,*
> *to the right degree,*
> *at the right time,*
> *for the right purpose,*
> *and in the right way —*
> *this is not easy."*

> *"The longer you keep your temper, the more it will improve."*
>
> Anonymous

4

CHAPTER 5

Make a Place for Yourself in the Nest

"No way! I was here first!"

"On some great hill of despair the bonfire you kindle can light the great sky — though it's true, of course, to make it burn you have to throw yourself in ... "

Galway Kinnell

"You seldom accomplish very much by yourself. You must get the assistance of others."

Henry J. Kaiser

To Make a Place for Yourself in This Nest, You May Have to Throw Yourself In

Isn't it unbelievable how hard you sometimes try to fit into a group? Have you ever done something really crazy to become a part of your nest? I certainly have.

What does a stepchick do to entertain three wild eggs and become a more solid part of the nest on a hot August night? I played (or tried to play) Rock Shark.

We walked the seven blocks from our home to the neighborhood park. In the middle of the park stands a "big toy." The big toy has a slide, a jungle gym, tire swings, ladders, crawl spaces and fort-like structures. It sits in the middle of a gravel space bordered by railroad ties, hence the name of the game, Rock Shark.

As the uninitiated player of this game, the rules had to be explained to me. (Steve had wisely decided to "just watch the game.") Stephanie began. "First, we choose the "shark." Ross

5

"Keep on going and chances are you will stumble on something, perhaps when you are least expecting it. I have never heard of anyone stumbling on something sitting down."

Charles F. Kettering

was chosen. He continued my instruction. "The object of the game is for the shark to go after somebody and tag them. Then that person is the shark." Cam concluded my orientation with, "The tricky part is that at no time may anyone's feet touch the 'rocks.'"

Wanting to participate fully, I then gave the usual adult-type warnings.

"Do not walk up the slide backwards. A slide is meant to be 'slidden' on."

"Be careful when crossing the ladder. Cross it using your hands, not your feet."

"Do not stand in the swings. Swings seats are specifically made for posteriors."

We called "time in" and the game began. Because this was my first time to play Rock Shark, I was the most vulnerable initial target for Ross. I frantically scrambled to escape him, trying to remember the rules (especially my own, modeling and all that jazz) as I flew around the big toy.

I successfully negotiated the fort area, crossed the ladder using my hands and suddenly realized that unless I ran up the slide backwards, I would have to touch the rocks or be caught. Of course, I broke the rules.

Scrambling up the slide with Ross in hot pursuit I attempted to gain speed by grabbing the metal bar at the top. In my haste and confusion, I thought the bar had a break in the middle. I assumed that I could pull myself through the space and scamper to the safety of the fort area.

To my utter shock, as I pulled myself up to the bar, there was no space in the middle. I pulled myself, full steam ahead, into the bar. Bar met bridge of nose with a resounding crunch. I actually heard the disgusting sound of my own nose breaking.

A blinding stab of pain shot through my upper sinus region. I struggled to hold on to the bar as I began to pass out. "I'm not going to pass out, fall off this thing and appear more ridiculous than I already do," I told myself as I struggled to stay conscious.

The kids were watching in amazement. How could anyone be that stupid? And then they saw the blood. Three kids panicked. Cam ripped off his shirt to catch the blood, Steph cried with me and Ross put his arms around me for comfort. Steve, watching from the safety of the grass, didn't know whether to be embarrassed or concerned.

Somehow we got me off the big toy and started on the walk back home. The conversation became slightly muddled. Steve kept saying, "Should I run and get the car? Can you make it?" Ross was muttering, "This is all my fault." Cam interjected, "No, it's my fault, I suggested the game," and Stephanie kept saying, "Does it hurt really bad, Rufeo?" With each step, more blood and pain made communication impossible. I finally blurted out, "I think I need to go to the emergency room."

What some stepchicks won't try to fit in!

What Is My Role in This Nest?

> *"It is not necessary to hope in order to undertake, nor to succeed in order to persevere."*
>
> Laurence J. Peter

You should ask yourself this question seriously before jumping into the nest and pushing and shoving to locate room for yourself. If you know the position you want, there will be fewer bruises for the nest at large.

Discuss your role with your spouse. Tell the eggs that you're not a replacement chick or rooster. Their biochick or rooster is very real and a part of their lives. Let the eggs know you're not attempting to push him out of their lives. He will not be a part of this nest, but he will still be a part of the chickenyard next door.

You could choose the role of "friend." That probably isn't the best choice.

What exactly does a "chickfriend" do when eggs are climbing the glass fixtures in a department store? Watch the faces of the saleschickens as they change from mild amazement to disgust? Say, "Now eggs, let's not do that?" You could do what I did. Change from friendchick to parentchick.

When the department store incident happened to me, the teacherchick instinct overcame the friendchick designation. I told the eggs, "Get down now and come over here." Then I placed those rotten eggs in time out on three of the four corners of the closest Oriental carpet. During their "think time," I lectured them about the benefits of being the type of egg(s) whom the chickenyard could like, respect and enjoy.

5

"Bear in mind, if you are going to amount to anything, that your success does not depend upon the brilliancy and the impetuosity with which you take hold, but upon the everlasting and sanctified bulldoggedness with which you hang on after you have taken hold."

Dr. A.B. Meldrum

I told Steve, "I have been disciplining other people's children for 17 years. Don't expect me to stop now!" After this incident, Steve, all three eggs and I believed me to be metamorphosing into the fairy tale wicked stepchick.

I was really confused. I felt I had done the right thing, and yet everybody in the nest disapproved of me at this moment. The rooster and the eggs didn't feel that I had acted as a friendchick at all. I hadn't acted as a friend I had acted as a parent. I had the undying respect and gratitude of the saleschickens, but they didn't live in my nest!

Steve and I began to have more conflicts, especially over disciplinary issues. I finally became so confused about what role I should play that we went to see a counselor. The counselor's advice was, "No matter how you try to avoid it, you're a parent figure. That means you have to participate in the family as a full member. It also means you have to discipline."

This advice was a relief and a centering point for both Steve and me. When we began to see me as a parentchick, work out how discipline was to be handled and reestablish my role with the eggs, things in our nest began changing for the better.

Who Does the Nest Want Me to Be?

Making the role decision on your own can lead to fried chickens and hard-boiled eggs. When you partner the nest in discussions, beginning with your spouse and expanding to the eggs, there is a comfort level with the decision that you come to together. This is called "ownership and partnering."

It has been so helpful to me to ask for nest opinions when I want to know something. I also wish that in the beginning, even though Stephanie was only four, I had asked each child and Steve what they wanted me to be instead of announcing what I was going to be.

Here is how I would do it today. I would ask these questions. Use them to help you discover what role the rest of the nest would be comfortable with, then negotiate your role.

I'm in This Nest to Stay.
What Do You Want Me to Be?

1. How would you like me to treat you?

_____

_____

_____

_____

_____

2. What do you think my part in this family is?

_____

_____

_____

_____

_____

3. What can I do to be your friend?

_____

_____

_____

_____

_____

There is Risk in Loving These Eggs

But there is another problem. Are you to create a relationship of your own with these eggs or simply be the facilitator of your spouse's relationship with them?

There is great risk in loving a stepegg. He may not love you back. You may never be as important to him as he is to you. But without the risk, there is never a chance to be a real squawking, wing-flapping, egg-cuddling part of the nest.

You may always wonder, "Whom does this egg love most?" Isn't it remarkable that eggs can love more than one adult chicken? Chickens can love more than one egg. Eggs and stepchickens struggle with the question, "Is there enough like or love to go around?"

"When you get into a tight place and everything goes against you, till it seems you could not hold on a minute longer, never give up then, for that is just the place and time that the tide will turn."

Harriet Beecher Stowe

> *"Fall seven times,*
> *stand up eight."*
>
> Japanese Proverb

My friend, Ruth Siress, also a stepchick, tells a wonderful story about one of her stepeggs. The little girl came home from kindergarten, and Ruth could tell by the swollen, puffy face that she had been crying. Ruth asked her, "What's wrong? Why are you upset?" She replied, "The kids at school have been asking me who I love more — you, or my biomom? I don't know what to tell them." In what Ruth describes as a message from God, she replied, "Honey, isn't it wonderful that love is not like a candy bar. You don't have to divide it in half for it to be equal. You can give all your love to your mom and you can give all your love to me."

Choose Your Role

Stepparenting is an active verb. You don't have to roost idly by while the members of the nest run amuck or shut you out. You don't have to let others define your role without your participation in this definition. You can choose to belong. You should actually feel fortunate because:

> **Birthing is a biological process**
> (It can happen to almost anyone.)
> ... but ...
>
> **Parenting is a conscious choice.**
> (Just because you're responsible for laying an egg doesn't mean you'll choose to parent it or hatch it well. Conversely, you don't have to lay an egg to decide to be a parent to it and hatch it or see it through to maturity.)

> *"Behold the turtle.*
> *He makes progress*
> *only when he sticks*
> *his neck out."*
>
> James B. Conant

By choosing a chicken with eggs to nest with, you're consciously choosing to parent these eggs. When you look at this as a choice you have made, you feel more in control and much more positive. You can write down what you think it means to be a parent. How should a chicken act toward these eggs? What does a parent do? What is a parent responsible for? Here is the list I made:

The Stepchicken's Ten Commandments of Egg-Hatching

1. A chicken teaches values.

2. A chicken knows the eggs.

3. A chicken likes the eggs.

4. A chicken helps the eggs treat others with respect.

5. A chicken builds self-esteem.

6. A chicken helps the egg discover who he is and gives freedom and space for discovery.

7. A chicken creates a motivational nest environment.

8. A chicken teaches responsibility.

9. A chicken protects the eggs (but not too much).

10. A chicken helps the egg live in the present and plan for the future.

A chicken models what she is teaching the eggs.

How will you do each of these things?" This "Live the Commandments Worksheet" will help you learn how to make these commandments part of your nest life.

Worksheet Purpose:

- To develop a list of role expectations for yourself as a parent
- To describe for yourself how you'll fulfill this role

"There is only one danger I find in life — you may take too many precautions."

Alfred Adler

5

5

> *"People who don't take risks generally make about two big mistakes a year. People who do take risks generally make about two big mistakes a year."*
>
> Peter Drucker

Worksheet Directions:

1. Develop your own parenting commandment list.

2. List ways that you can live your role commandments.

3. Ask your spouse to develop his/her own commandment list independently.

4. Compare, negotiate and consolidate lists.

5. Take into consideration the feedback from the eggs in the "What Do You Want Me to Be?" sheet.

6. Realize that creating these commandments can be done at any point in your nesting experience.

7. When you have made your list and applications, post it.

8. Begin living the list.

Example:

Commandment 2. A parent knows the child.

Commandment Application:

I will plan times when this child and I can do specific activities that will help me know him better. I will ask this child what he most likes to do. I will offer to do this activity with this child.

I will arrange to go to this child's classroom at school and observe. I will eat lunch with this child and meet some of his friends.

I will listen when this child comes home from school and wants to tell me about his day. I will ask questions that will help me know more.

Live the Commandments

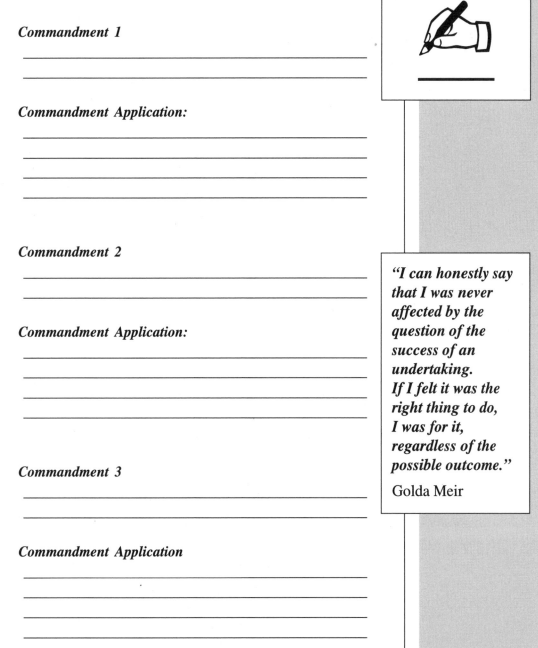

Commandment 1

_____

_____

Commandment Application:

_____

_____

_____

_____

Commandment 2

_____

_____

Commandment Application:

_____

_____

_____

_____

Commandment 3

_____

_____

Commandment Application

_____

_____

_____

_____

> *"I can honestly say that I was never affected by the question of the success of an undertaking. If I felt it was the right thing to do, I was for it, regardless of the possible outcome."*
>
> Golda Meir

5

5

Commandment 4

_____

_____

Commandment Application

_____

_____

_____

_____

Commandment 5

_____

_____

Commandment Application

_____

_____

_____

_____

"The only place success comes before work is in the dictionary."

Donald Kendall

Summary: We're All in This Coop Together

You have freely chosen to become a part of the life of your spouse. That means you have also freely chosen to have his eggs in your life. Few nests begin with smiling eggs and chickens, and there are few nest-construction blueprints. By working together to define roles, you can run a smoother, more understanding chickenyard where emotionally healthy chickens and eggs can coexist.

You have many things in common in this nest. Fear of crushed eggs, scorched chickens and a battered nest are common feelings for eggs and chickens. Open expression of these feelings both positive and negative help the nest to realize, "Hey, those other yardbirds are worried about this, too."

Even the eggs realize how hard it can be for a chick or a rooster to fit in. Sometimes they look back with gratitude for the attempt. This poem, written by an adult stepdaughter as a special Mother's Day Tribute to her stepmother, describes with heartbreaking tenderness this life we choose when we choose to parent the other chick's eggs.

Mother of the Year

They came in not two,
or three, or four,
but five little girls
walked through that door.
Their hearts filled with sadness,
questions and fears,
at the changes surrounding them
which had brought many tears.
They were met by a woman
who had chosen a new life,
to be there, to care,
to help them all through the strife.
The road wasn't easy
for this new kindred clan.
There was testing, defying,
and challenges to this plan.
But a special woman,
with patience, caring and trust,
knew their needs were great,
so to weather the storm was a must.
She was cook and housekeeper,
chauffeur, nurse and wife.
She turned a house to a home
and created a haven for their life.
Someone who chooses to care,
teach and share,
who weathers the storms by choice,
is a gem so precious and rare.
She embodies the meaning of friend,
confidant and mother.

"I studied the lives of great men and famous women, and I found that the men and women who got to the top were those who did the jobs they had in hand, with everything they had of energy and enthusiasm and hard work."

Harry S. Truman

5

5

> *"It is not enough for parents to understand children. They must accord children the privilege of understanding them."*
>
> Milton R. Sapirstein

She's a treasure, a prize, a gift like no other.
I don't tell her enough,
but I want her to know today
she could never be replaced
she's a part of my life that was meant to stay.
A very treasured place
she holds deep in my heart.
She is woven into the fabric of me, never to part.
So on this special day
made to honor someone who is dear
I dedicate this poem
to my "Mother of the Year."

Mother's Day 1996

Reproduced by permission.
©1996, Jeannette Ford

"I have spread my dreams under your feet: tread softly because you tread on my dreams."

W.B. Yeats

*C*HAPTER 6

Feathering the Nest with High Self-Esteem

"I like me, I like you. RIGHT!"

"I have woven a parachute out of everything broken."
William Stafford

Untying Nest Knots

I was walking along the sidewalk recently and noticed a worm who actually had himself tied in a knot. He was working so hard to free himself that he was beginning to make some headway. I kind of chuckled and walked back to help him out of his mess.

Seeing the worm in his predicament reminded me of how we looked and felt as a group in the beginning of our stepfamily experience. We were tied in knots. Our nest was a hard place to grow because we were each so wrapped up in our knots that we were concerned only with getting untied individually. That left us little or no time to relate meaningfully as a group.

One of the worst knots for stepfamilies to untie is the knot of self-esteem. Each egg and the rooster and chick are working on individual self-esteem. But then there's the matter of nest self-esteem.

Esteem issues are common in every family. However, these issues become compounded for stepfamilies. Inside the nest, the eggs say to themselves, "There must be something wrong with me because my parents split up." "There must be something wrong with me. My stepparent doesn't like me."

"Responsibility, n. A detachable burden easily shifted to the shoulders of God, Fate, Fortune, luck or one's neighbor. In the days of astrology, it was customary to unload it upon a star."

Ambrose Bierce

> *"Do what you can, with what you have, where you are."*
>
> Theodore Roosevelt

6

The chick and rooster have inner messages which say, "There must be something wrong with me that I couldn't make my marriage work." "There must be something wrong with me. These kids don't like me."

The entire nest asks, "Why isn't our family like everyone else's?"

You also have the yardbirds' comments to deal with. Comments such as, "Well, in a *normal* nest" "You're not the biochick/rooster ..." "You'll never be a biological nest" "I can't *believe* you thought *that* would work." With comments such as these, the nest becomes even more knotted.

Your individual self-doubt threatens your happiness as individual chickens and eggs and as nestmates. You read books, magazines and the publications of self-help groups that reinforce your self-doubt. They tell you, "You cannot and will not function as a biological family." "You cannot replace the biological parent." With everyone telling you what you're not, you need to find out what and who you are. How do you escape feeling second, used, not perfect, resulting from mistakes?

When I thought about the self-esteem of our nest and tried to think of examples of broken eggs, a frazzled chick or a warped-out rooster, all I could remember was the good stuff. Wasn't it just last night Stephanie said, "I can't think of anything about myself that I don't like"? Just last week Ross said, "I have so many friends!" I began to feel pretty good about us. Then the fertilizer began flying across my mind:

Cam's jaw muscle tightening and releasing as he sat paralyzed with fear and self-doubt after encountering and walking away from a bully;

Working on a self-esteem program with Ross when, as a fifth grader, both his classroom teacher and his gifted and talented teacher said he was becoming a negative leader and they suspected low self-esteem;

Listening to Stephanie's teacher say that Steph couldn't make decisions on her own and was asking for help with even simple tasks;

Hearing Steve say to the kids, "You did too do that. I saw you. What do think I am, stupid? I am not stupid!"

Remembering myself saying, "Do not make one more comment on how much I eat. I do not eat too much. I just eat the wrong things!"

As I write this, I have just come from the kitchen, where Ross has done two things we have asked him to do.

He has actually emptied the dishwasher after doing a load of dishes and placed the beginning of the next load in the washer.

He has made a grocery list and left it on the kitchen counter where we can find it.

These things may not seem like self-esteem miracles to you, but they are responsibilities we have been working on for some time. We have found that working together for the good of the nest has created feelings of high self-esteem for us as eggs, chick and rooster separately and as a nest together. By the way, not only did Ross leave these lists in plain sight, taped to the counter, but he also added his own personal flair by signing one of them, "By Ross the Great," a fair indication of high esteem for an individual egg.

Of course, this chick was so thrilled that she had to add her own touches of stickers on his notes, saying things like, "Super," "Great job," "Thanks for helping out," and "You make me smile." When eggs feel good enough about themselves to remember to help others, it gives chicks and roosters esteem-building opportunities.

So how do you continue getting the knots out of your nest? How do you work on developing a flock with high self- and group esteem?

> *"The way to learn any game is to play for more than you can afford to lose."*
>
> Anonymous

Feather the Nest to Keep from Getting Plucked

6

Sometimes eggs, chicks and roosters pluck at themselves. Sometimes the yardbirds do the plucking of individual nest members and the whole nest. How does the nest feather itself to keep from getting plucked?

Five Feathers for the Nest:

1. The Identity Feather

2. The Positive Clucking Feather

3. The Responsibility Feather

4. The Respect Feather

5. The Pride Feather

Here are some of the ways you can work on each of these five feathers.

1. The Identity Feather

It has been easier for the kids to find this feather because they have grown up in a culture that talks freely about esteem. From the first schoolyard years, eggs have been trained to value who they are. This is harder for chicks and roosters who were taught things like, "Eggs are to be seen and not heard."

A very good learning, enlightening and eventually healing exercise for you is to each create a life collage. You will learn about yourselves and each other. Here's how you do it.

A. Get a large sheet of newsprint or poster board.
B. You may draw, use cut-outs or a combination of both.
C. Use these pictures to represent the happy and sad times in your life, now and in the past.

D. You may also use actual pictures of people you know, places you have been and things that have helped you become who you are today.

E. You may include cut-out or written words.

F. Objects may also be placed in your collage.

G. Smaller eggs usually like this activity. Even if they can't read yet, they can understand when you ask them questions such as:

    1. Who is a person you really like?

    2. What is your favorite toy?

    3. What is the color you like best?

    4. Which room of our home is your most comfortable place?

    5. What is your favorite thing to do in the summer?

H. Eggs, chicks and roosters like to use any pictures that represent birth, early childhood, adolescence, teen years and young adulthood.

I. Nest members should be encouraged to have this collage be one that is a personal history.

What you get is a better personal understanding of who you are as unique members of the flock and how you have become who you are. You understand better how life events work together to influence what you become. You get an added benefit of finding differences and similarities in your past nests. For example: As our family shared our collages, there were moments of revelation. When my collage included a picture representing a really scary experience with a bully egg in the seventh grade, Cam realized he was not alone in his fear after his experience with a bully.

Your next helpful discovery activity is the worksheet, " About Myself."

> *"Where parents do too much for their children, the children will not do much for themselves."*
>
> Elbert Hubbard

6

About Myself

1. When do you like yourself most?

   _____

   _____

   _____

2. Where are you when you feel best about yourself?

   _____

   _____

   _____

3. Who are you with when you feel best about yourself?

   _____

   _____

   _____

4. What activities do you do best?

   _____

   _____

   _____

5. What's the nicest thing anyone's ever said about you? Who said it?

   _____

   _____

   _____

6. What has been your proudest moment?

   _____

   _____

   _____

7. What makes you happy?

   _____

   _____

   _____

"Lend yourself to others, but give yourself to yourself."

Michel de Montaigne

8. What would you like to learn more about?

    _____
    _____
    _____

9. Who are your three best friends?

    _____
    _____
    _____

10. What makes you feel bad about yourself?

    _____
    _____
    _____

11. Who are you with when you feel worst about yourself?

    _____
    _____
    _____

12. If I could have three wishes that would come true, they would be:

    _____
    _____
    _____

13. The best present I've ever received was

    _____
    _____
    _____

14. My favorite teacher was/is

    _____
    _____
    _____

"You cannot climb uphill by thinking downhill thoughts."

Anonymous

6

6

15. If I were a gift, I would be

_____

_____

_____

16. Ten years from now I will probably be

_____

_____

_____

17. Ten years from now I will own

_____

_____

_____

18. In ten years, I think these changes will probably take place

_____

_____

_____

19. What makes your heart sing?

_____

_____

_____

20. What makes your heart cry?

_____

_____

_____

> *"For everything you have missed, you have gained something else."*
>
> Anonymous

The "About Myself" worksheet is a variation of sheets I used to use in teaching. Even the toughest, hardest-to-reach kids always enjoyed filling out these sheets. Steve, the kids and I learned a lot about ourselves and each other as we filled them out.

In addition to the "About Myself" worksheet, here's another one from which the entire nest can grow. The "How Do You Feel?" worksheet. There are no "what this means" or "what category do my answers put me in?" scales. This is an information gauge, not a test.

How Do You Feel?

Rate how you feel about yourself in each of these categories.

1 means you don't have much of this.
10 means you have a lot of this.

Smart	1	2	3	4	5	6	7	8	9	10
Attractive	1	2	3	4	5	6	7	8	9	10
Personable	1	2	3	4	5	6	7	8	9	10
Hard Worker										
At home	1	2	3	4	5	6	7	8	9	10
At school/work	1	2	3	4	5	6	7	8	9	10
Good Listener	1	2	3	4	5	6	7	8	9	10
Efficient	1	2	3	4	5	6	7	8	9	10
Responsible	1	2	3	4	5	6	7	8	9	10
Respectful	1	2	3	4	5	6	7	8	9	10
Committed	1	2	3	4	5	6	7	8	9	10
Courteous	1	2	3	4	5	6	7	8	9	10
Achiever	1	2	3	4	5	6	7	8	9	10
Well-dressed	1	2	3	4	5	6	7	8	9	10
Well-groomed	1	2	3	4	5	6	7	8	9	10
Organized	1	2	3	4	5	6	7	8	9	10
Flexible	1	2	3	4	5	6	7	8	9	10

"Morale is when your hands and feet keep on working when your head simply says it can't be done."

Anonymous

6

After each member of the flock works on this gauge individually, compare notes as a flock. Then look at this gauge again sometime when you are feeling bad about yourselves. Look back at your strengths for an instant chicken-smile.

Another way to feel like flying is to look at an item like "well-dressed." If being well-dressed or well-groomed makes you feel good, then when you're feeling at the bottom of the coop, you can use this knowledge to know what might help you feel like flying again.

6

2. The Positive Clucking Feather.

Have you ever added up the positive things you cluck about each day and then added up the negative things you cluck about? What do you think your ratio of positive to negative clucks would be? Many members of the yard are "fowl" in their clucking.

It seems to be much easier to be negative about yourself and others than to be positive. The trouble is, the barnyard begins to smell pretty bad when negatives overflow it. Too much fertilizer is not a good thing. It begins to drown living things.

It takes 12 positive clucks to overcome one negative cluck. Much of the negative clucking you do is to yourself about yourself. You cluck over 1,200 words per minute to yourself. What are you saying when you cluck to yourself about yourself? When you do something incorrectly, do you say, "Boy, am I stupid or what? That was a really dumb thing to do"? Or do you say, "I really learned from that yard experience. Here's how I'll handle that one next time"?

If you are really used to clucking to yourself negatively, it's a hard habit to break. I shared with my eggs something that I have done for 10 years to help myself cluck to me more positively. My first marriage was to an emotionally and verbally abusive person. Even after years of support from my family as I grew up, when I was around this clucker, who told me almost everything I did was wrong, I began to think of myself as a pretty dumb chick. After being married to this banty rooster for 11 years and constantly being beaten down, I needed a building-up program.

Here's the way I build myself up. When I want to feel good about myself or get better at doing something, I simply say:

> "I want to ... ."
> "I can ... ."
> "I am ... ."

I began by saying...

> "I want to be a good person."
> "I can be a good person."
> "I am a good person."

Right now I'm working on "I am on time." I have 3x5 cards on my computer work station and in my car that say this. It's the "I am..." part that you can put in front of yourselves daily to help you improve by refocusing your thoughts to positive clucking.

I discovered that one of my eggs was watching what I was doing pretty closely. That egg was Stephanie. Stephanie was the only girl playing baseball in Kansas City last year. She could hit any ball pitched to her by a pitching machine. She could hit any ball pitched to her by her coach. But when she stood in the batter's box in a real game, she couldn't hit the ball if it was tied to her bat! Her coach had told her that she was going to be the best second baseperson that team had ever had.

Stephanie came to me and said, "I'm never going to get a chance to play second base if I can't hit the ball during the game." I said, "Steph, why can't you hit the ball during the game when you can always hit it in the batting cage or when Coach is pitching to you?" She said, "Rufeo, those boys in the dugout say, 'Girls can't hit.'" I said, "Steph, what do you think you should do about this problem?" She said, "I need one of those cards."

She went to my desk and got a 3x5 card. She wrote, "I am a great hitter." She tacked it up on the wall in her bedroom. In a few minutes she came back to me and said, "What if I need to see this during the game?" I said, "You need to be creative, don't you?" She was. She wrote another, "I am a great hitter" card and tucked it in the inside lining of her baseball cap.

It took her several days to talk her coach into sending her back into the game. I could see her studying the inside of her cap in the dugout. She finally got up to bat. Strike one. Strike two. The third ball is pitched. Stephanie swung. Her bat connected with that ball and she hit a runner home. She made it to third base herself.

We had not taken Steph to the batting cages any more than we usually did. Her coach had not worked with her any harder than he usually did. She simply changed her own mind by changing to positive clucking.

Each of you can have "I am" cards for whatever negative clucking you are working on changing . You improve by teaching yourself to think positively, focus on the issue and cluck kindly to yourself.

> *"The ability to accept responsibility is the measure of the man."*
>
> Roy L. Smith

6

6

3. The Responsibility Feather.

Blaming becomes a very common part of yard behavior in a stepnest. Biochicks and roosters blame each other. Eggs blame bioeggs and stepeggs. The yard blames the biofamily of each member of the nest, and the nest members blame themselves quietly and everyone else out loud.

Blaming behavior creates a negative nest that really ties itself in knots. Blaming behavior does not make a coop run smoothly. It simply causes the fertilizer piles to get higher.

As a member of a stepnest, it is especially easy for eggs to say when confronted with unacceptable behavior at home, school, church or anywhere else, "I can't help it. I live in a stepnest," or "I'm not responsible for that. I grew up in a stepnest." This can produce a chicken who never takes responsibility for any flapping. This becomes a great excuse for ruffled feathers. It's much easier to blame other members of the yard or yard conditions than to face having to take personal responsibility.

I know biochicks and roosters who do not discipline. They choose to wait until one of their eggs exhibits a behavior that is undesirable, attempt to discipline, haven't tried it before so the egg chirps disrespectfully, then take the egg to a counselor, saying, "He lies," and expect the counselor to "fix it." This is not only a perfect example of eggpassing, but of blame fixing. The biochick or rooster is the one with the problem but attempts to pass it off as the egg's problem.

How could you teach personal responsibility to eggs and get them to practice it? Start very simply with "I" messages.

I had talked with Ross about the fact that his response to anything that upset him was crying about it. We discussed that crying is an inappropriate response to many things. We talked about how taking action to solve the problem is a much more responsible behavior than crying, especially if by crying you feel you can manipulate the outcome. Eggs in stepnests watch the chicks and roosters in both nests attempt to manipulate each other and learn to imitate this type of negative squawking very well.

The first few discussions resulted in Ross saying, "Well, Cameron made me cry. He made me angry." We worked on getting him to say instead, "I chose to cry because that's how

I am showing my anger." I explained that when Ross tells Cam, "You made me cry," he also tells Cam, "You have the power to make me cry." You say to yourself instead, "I don't choose to give anyone this power over me. I can choose not to cry."

Turn this into a personal-responsibility contract. Add a few steps to help the egg in thinking this through. Here's an example of steps you need to take to keep the egg from cracking.

> *"Lack of something to feel important about is almost the greatest tragedy a man may have."*
>
> Arthur E. Moraan

6

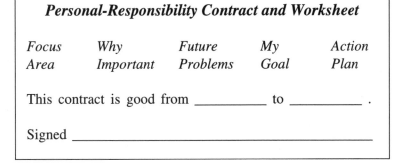

Personal-Responsibility Contract and Worksheet

Focus Area	*Why Important*	*Future Problems*	*My Goal*	*Action Plan*

This contract is good from _____ to _____ .

Signed _____

Here's how a finished contract might look:

Personal Responsibility Contract and Worksheet

Focus Area	*Why Important*	*Future Problems*	*My Goal*	*Action Plan*
Anger Crying	Self-control Self-confidence Self-image Image to others	Remembering Taking time out Self-control Doing it	Find a more appropriate anger response	1) When I feel angry enough to cry, I will say to myself "time out." 2) I will take a deep breath. 3) I will say, "I am responsible for my actions. I can choose not to cry."

This contract is good from __6/1__ to __7/1__ .

Signed_Ross Henry Clurman_

A Coop Responsibility Feather Practice Move

To begin acting on taking personal responsibility instead of blaming others, do this activity.

Think about a time when something went wrong. You wanted to blame someone else. Write about it here.

_____

_____

_____

_____

_____

6

> *"Responsibility educates."*
>
> Wendell Phillips

4. The Respect Feather.

A stepnest is a very tough place to build respect. Respect for other yard members is certainly not commonly modeled by biochicks and roosters or stepchicks and roosters when dealing with the other nest. Eggs can come out very scrambled on this issue of respect.

Beginning a stepnest by teaching respect can be the smartest thing you do. When each nest member respects the space of other members, this prevents squawking about privacy invasions. When each nest member respects differences in habits and ideas, this prevents clashes over who is really flying the "right" way. After many such chicken-fights over invasions and the correct way to fly, our family motto is now, "Treat each egg, chick or rooster with respect."

As a new nest member who had lived for five years in a nest by myself, I was frustrated with the squawking that happened among eggs. After my years of being married to a verbal abuser, squawking is something that really fries this chick. It makes life very unpleasant for all other members of the yard. I had tried clucking about this problem and had laid an egg. I decided a new strategy was needed to produce respect in the nest.

Finally, I came upon the nest-motto idea. A nest mission statement can help you begin to fly in the same direction and avoid crashing in take-off attempts. A nest mission statement is reinforced through constant repetition. For example: Two years ago we bought what we call "the conflict-resolution vehicle."

When I became a parent at the age of 40, I was reminded of something I had forgotten since childhood. When eggs' elbows touch in cars, there is conflict. We bought a van. The main feature we were interested in were captain's seats all the way back. We explained that this should give each egg ample wing room. If an egg happened to invade another egg's nesting area, then the nest mission statement should automatically kick in.

We were doing well until one day when Cameron and Stephanie and I were riding along. I was driving; Cam and Steph were seated in the very back. All of a sudden the Steph-Siren went off. "Ca-a-a-amero-o-o-on!" I said, "Are we treating each egg with respect?" Cameron said, "Yes." Stephanie said, "NO!" "All right, let's debrief this," I said. (They know what this means. Their stepchick is a trainer!) "Cam, you go first." "All I did was ask her can I use her Walkman." "That sounds reasonable," I said. "Steph, what's the problem?" "Rufeo, he didn't wait for me to answer. He snatched it!" Would you say that these are two eggs with a definitional difference? Cam abides by the letter of the respect law. He asks permission. Stephanie assumes the intent of the respect law is to also wait for an answer before snatching!

That led to the next phase of problem-solving. Use these worksheets to define what each of you mean by respect.

*"Not in the clamor of the crowded street,
Not in the shouts and plaudis of the throng,
But in ourselves, are triumph and defeat."*

Longfellow

6

95

6

Nest Respect Worksheet

Nest Mission Statement: *"Treat each egg, chick or rooster with respect."*

Instructions: *On this worksheet list each nest member's name. List the things this member of the nest could do to cause you to feel that he/she is treating you with respect.*

Your name _____

Name _____

Name _____

Name _____

Name _____

Name _____

Name _____

After completing the "Nest Respect Worksheet," you then go to the "Nest Respect Contract." Each nest member has a respect contract with each other nest member. Some contracts are more complicated and terse than others. Some nest members have more trouble avoiding pushing each other out than others. Here's what the contract looks like:

Nest Respect Contract

Agreement between _____ and

_____ .

Date: _____

I Will	**You Will**
_____	_____

Here's an example of what the bioeggs' (Cam's and Ross's) contract looked like:

6

Respect Contract
Ross / Cam

(Ross's part)
I will:

1. Let you do whatever you want your own way
2. Not bug you by acting weird
3. Let you tell me something without me interrupting you while you are talking
4. Not mess with your things
5. Not wear your clothes (when I know they are yours)
6. Not look over your shoulder

(Cam's part)
You will:

1. Not hit me, push me or bump me for no reason.
2. Stop the first time I ask you to
3. Not try to get me to get rough with you by bugging me
4. Tell the truth without stretching it
5. Not spy on me

We will honor this *Respect Contract*.

My signature:

_____

Your signature:

_____

"It isn't that they can't see the solution. It is that they can't see the problem."

G.K. Chesterton

6

Then suddenly, out of no-nest-land, with no prompting from the chick or rooster, "Rules for Cam's Room" appeared. The eggs soon figured out: if it's written down, it's fair. If it's written down, those eggs feel less defensive.

Here are the "Rules for Cam's Room":

Rules for Cam's Room

1. Do not get into my dresser without asking (It's OK for Dad and R-A.).

2. If you're going to play with something, please put it back!

3. If you want to borrow some of my clothes, ask first.

4. Please do not jump on my bed!

5. Do not throw anything unless I am there to catch it.

6. Please do not scratch my walls.

7. Do not eat or drink anything in there without permission.

8. IF MY DOOR IS SHUT, PLEASE KNOCK FIRST!!!

9. Make sure your feet are clean before you come in.

10. If you want to use my phone and I'm not home, don't make long-distance phone calls. If I am home, please ask me before using it.

11. If you break something, please contact me immediately. If you can't get ahold of me, tell me as soon as you see me.

12. Do not use my colognes or my deodorants without asking.

13. If you want to listen to my radio, make sure you turn it off when you're through.

14. MAKE SURE YOU TURN THE LIGHT OUT WHEN YOU LEAVE MY ROOM!!!!!!!!

Respect is a major feather for nest members. The next big challenge for your nest will be remembering to extend this feather outside the walls of your nest into the larger coop and yard. It's a tough modeling job for chicks and roosters, but it also reminds you to slow down and think in difficult situations with difficult bio or stepchicks and roosters.

6

5. The Pride Feather

A real test for the nest to see if the knots are coming untied is this: Can you recognize and celebrate successes? This is a huge chicken step past simply thinking of ways to pluck the other members of the flock. Celebrating is real nest-feathering.

> *"Every noble work is at first impossible."*
> Thomas Carlyle

We celebrate success in our nest. We experience success because we work so hard at it. Some of our most important individual successes have been:

Cameron completed his eighth grade year with a perfect 4.0 grade average. Not only that, but he had the highest grade average in the entire eighth grade.

Ross completed a 4.0 last quarter and scored in the top eight percent of the nation on the Iowa Basic Skills Test.

Stephanie was the only girl playing baseball in the City Little League.

Steve has opened his own drive-through or sit-in gourmet coffee shop, achieving a lifetime goal of owning his own business.

Ruth-Ann met income and sales goals that she set for herself when she opened her own consulting business two years ago and continues to be satisfied and fulfilled in her work.

None of these things happened by accident. We set goals and focused on meeting them. We supported each other in these goals and celebrated when they were met. We celebrated with special dinners, special events, cards, balloons, lots of hugging, smiles and "I'm really proud of you's."

Here's a worksheet you can use to celebrate your nest successes.

6

Pride Day

There are many things that members of this nest do to make me proud to be a nest member. Sometimes I forget to tell each nest member why I want to crow. This is my chance to crow about each of you.

I would like to crow about...

Name _____

because _____

_____

_____

Name _____

because _____

_____

_____

Name _____

because _____

_____

_____

Name _____

because _____

_____

_____

Name _____

because _____

_____

_____

Name _____

because _____

_____

_____

Feathering the Nest Summary

Feathering the nest instead of getting plucked takes real determination and cooperation. Each of you will continue to struggle with self-esteem issues. Each of you will continue to be strengthened by the struggle as you determine not to let the yard take your feathers.

A real cautionary note: Don't contribute to your own plucking by negative squawking. Each of you will support the others in this struggle, and each of you will continue to be proud of and celebrate the success of the others in the nest.

Nests are feathered one feather at a time. Each feather used strengthens the ones that come after it. The more you pile up feathers, the less the chances of getting plucked.

Challenge each member of your nest to build with these five feathers.

W.S. Merwin has said, *"We are asleep with compasses in our hands."* Using these five feathers will get the nest to wake up and use the compasses to succeed as stepnests.

> *"We are asleep with compasses in our hands."*
>
> W.S. Merwin

6

101

6

C HAPTER 7

Breed Nest Resistance to Chaos and Stress

One of many Maalox moments!

"Time is the scarcest resource, and unless it is managed nothing else can be managed."

Peter Drucker

"Time is the scarcest resource, and unless it is managed nothing else can be managed."

Peter Drucker

A Nest Short on Time Management Will Be a Stressed Nest

Do peaceful mornings that are happy, self-actualizing, sharing times rather than rude wake-up calls sound like a dream? Do evenings that are quietly productive seem impossible? Do you ever wish that family projects could be bonding experiences instead of war zones? Does stress ooze from every pore of your stepfamily experience?

You are all stuck in the nest together. What can you do, even in the sometimes abbreviated time you are together as a stepnest, to ease stress by managing time well?

When I taught school, I had a successful, ordered classroom. I accomplished this by partnering my students in setting the agenda for projects. We would simply discuss what needed to be done, set a plan for doing it and achieve a relatively stress-free, successful project completion.

> *"Time is everything. Anything you want, anything you accomplish — pleasure, success, fortune — is measured in time."*
>
> Joyce C. Hall

When I became a stepparent, I assumed that this process would work well with my new nest. The first week that I had the eggs all to myself because Steve was on a business trip, we sat down on Sunday night to discuss how Monday morning could be a stress-free nest for each of us.

We talked about all eggs needing to be in the van by seven. I asked if each egg knew exactly what he/she had to do to accomplish that. Each egg said, "Yes," (with confidence). I assumed that we were all on the same page and that seven o'clock Monday morning, all would be peaceful and we would be on our way to work and school. Now I know why, though I loved my school kids, I never had the urge to take any of them home with me!

Monday morning was a complete disaster. There was squawking, pushing, spilled cereal, two eggs who forgot to make a lunch, and at 7:15 a.m. we were still looking for shoes. We finally got in the van with a minimum number of cracked eggs about 7:30. I was devastated! My first opportunity to have a really smooth nest with no interference from Steve was not going well at all. I looked in the rearview mirror at the fractured eggs, checked my mirror and found one overdone chick and said, "Well. Was any of that fun?" Cam said, "Are you kidding?"

It suddenly dawned on me that I was on my way to Hallmark to teach time management! In desperation, I decided to find out if anything I was teaching at work might help in the nest. I spent my lunch hour converting retail-store time management to nest time management.

I prepared forms for each flock member to fill out about what activities we needed to consider as we got ready for school and work in the morning. I also prepared forms for returning to the nest activities in the evening. I sat everyone down as soon as we got securely in the nest and said, "This morning was a disaster!" To choruses of, "You got that right," and "It was awful. Ross made me spill my cereal, and I was the one who got in trouble for it." I outlined what we needed to do to have a more successful and less stressful morning. I also explained that we needed to work on evening activity schedules because that would help us accomplish all that we needed to do at night with some time left to do what we wanted to do.

To my utter surprise, the eggs were enthusiastic about preparing the time schedules. They were even more enthusiastic about the opportunity to make their own lunches each evening as part of the time success plan. To create the schedules, I asked them to list everything they could think of that they needed to do from the time they heard the cock crow until the time they stepped into the van. Then they listed each thing they needed to do from the time we walked in the door at night until the time they went to roost.

After these lists were completed, they organized them in chronological order and wrote beside each item how long they thought it would take to do that activity. Then we had a reality check because Stephanie said it would take her five minutes to brush her teeth. With comments such as, "Your dentist wishes," I helped them revise their time estimates to real numbers. Then we added up how much time each egg needed in the morning and in the evening. We created back-off schedules based on the time we had to get in the van in the a.m. and bed time in the p.m.

They set their own alarms for their wake-up time, made their own lunches for the first time (we talked about food groups and healthy choices), practiced their p.m. schedule for the first time and trotted off to roost cheerfully. They followed their schedules to perfection. What's more, they were happy about it because they had some control over their activities. They also were learning immediately how much better it feels to plan, set goals, have a schedule and be able to measure accomplishments.

Tuesday morning, each egg had his schedule that we had typed up on the computer posted by his doorway in the nest. Each egg (including Steph, who was six at the time) had the responsibility for running his own schedule without beady eyes interfering.

One of the things the eggs liked best about the schedule was that each egg could set his own order of doing things. The only thing which had to be coordinated and negotiated when making the schedules was taking showers.

I kept listening for the sounds of the squawking I had heard on Monday morning. I got worried and checked several times because the nest was so quiet. Each time I checked, the eggs were quietly progressing toward getting dressed and eating breakfast. Part of the quiet came from the intense personal-schedule checking to make certain each egg was on track.

> *"The American people are so tense that it is impossible to put them to sleep — even with a sermon."*
>
> Norman Vincent Peale

> *"Most misfortunes are the results of misused time."*
>
> Napoleon Hill

Ross is the notorious late egg, and he knows it. Because of this, he and I had devised the strategy of a timer. He set the timer for each new activity phase and tried to beat it. Even he was on schedule!

At 6:50 a.m., the eggs were in the van. At 6:55, they came looking for me asking, "What's your problem? Are you going to make it? You said doughnuts if we all got to the van on time. Does that mean you too?"

By 7:00 a.m., peacefully, all clothes on (and on straight), breakfast cleaned up, all lunches and backpacks in place, we were on our way! Wow! The first morning, a complete success! I asked, "How does it feel different today than yesterday?" Ross said, "I'm not stressed out, and you didn't have to get mad at me." Steph said, "I didn't spill anything. Ross wasn't even in the kitchen when I was eating." Cam said, "You know I love schedules. It makes me feel organized and peaceful." (This from the West Point Wanna-Be.)

Our afternoon schedule also went smoothly, and we even had time to watch a TV show together and read before heading to roost. We made it peacefully through Wednesday (both schedules), and by Thursday morning, we were a happy, well-functioning, fairly stress-free nest team. One of the kids even said, "I wish my teacher would use our time plan."

Thursday night, Steve came back to the nest. Friday morning Ross came to me and said, "Ruth-Ann, Dad is messing up the schedule." I said, "Well, he wasn't here when we made it. Can you show him what we did and teach him to make one for himself?" Ross said, "I sure hope so!" (Steve continues to have his own version of time management, but the rest of us get it down so smoothly that it works even with Steve's original interpretations.)

Beat Nest Stress with Pro-Active Time Planning

One of the reasons stress occurs is that in the short and long times you spend together you haven't planned how the time will be spent. Of course, there's room for spontaneity, but when you don't plan together, different mental agendas fly into each other, and crushed eggs and fried chickens result. Eggs plan to play with neglected toys or "veg out." The rooster had plans for a work day in the yard with evening trips to the hiking trail and bike rides. The chick plans for some pleasant outing followed by a movie, and each of you have different ideas about what to have for meals and when to eat.

You will find that negotiated planning which starts with a list of possible activities prepared and thought out by the rooster and the chick makes for a greater chance of success in your times together. Options are presented and negotiated, and sometimes you can even vote. Eggs have learned to speak up in phone calls during the week about what they might like to do.

Expectations are met because you have a plan. Time management works to reduce stress for you.

Making your lists and posting them, outlining activities in writing and preparing "job descriptions" of each task place you in greater control of your outcomes and reduce your stress and conflict.

Each of the Tip Sheets, Schedule Sheets, Job Descriptions, Contracts, and To-Do Lists included are designed to guide you as you orchestrate a more peaceful stepnest through time and stress management.

7

> *"Dost thou love life, then do not squander time, for that's the stuff life is made of."*
>
> Benjamin Franklin

7

Enhance Nest Security and Structure with Activity Time Management

Another reason that the planned approach to time spent together works well in a stepnest is that it brings a measure of structure and security. When the lists are posted for all to see and the planned/negotiated activities are a constant of time together, it increases the ease of transition from nest to nest because you know that the first thing after greeting each other and catching up on time away is planning for this time together.

This planning can ease Nest Transition Stress because it gives you something you know you're going to talk about. Even after nest members become familiar with each other, the "What do I say first?" time can be awkward.

Here's an example of a preplanned choice for activities.

Nest Activity Advance Preparation Sheet
or
Things We Could Do for Fun Tonight

1. Go see (movie choice 1).
2. Go see (movie choice 2).
3. Bake cookies.
4. Work with a craft.
5. Rent a video.

All of the above include eating dinner at our choice of:
* McDonald's
* Winstead's
* Food Court at the mall
* Pizza Hut

What'll it be, eggs?

Passing out these papers with the choices written on them gives the eggs something to do immediately. It takes their minds off transition time and gets them right into some interesting choices. Any nest member who chooses not to participate automatically agrees to go along with the flock choice without ruffled feathers showing.

Votes can be done silently by circling items that are chosen. This reduces loud noises and attempts to influence other eggs.

You can prepare the list of activities that are possibilities yourselves as the chick and rooster and/or you can let the eggs take turns preparing them a week or two in advance. This gives the eggs real input individually and gives you real clues as to what each individual egg would really like to do. When the eggs do the planning, it is with the understanding that it will be something each nest member could appreciate and enjoy. It is also with the understanding that each egg gets a turn.

Eggs can either prepare advance plans that have choices or they can have the option of preparing an activity as the only choice. They just have to plan the activity thoroughly with the help of a chick or rooster. ·

Exercise: Do a Nest Activity Advance Preparation Sheet.

Nest Activity Preparation Sheet

Instructions: Each time a nest member has an idea for a nest activity or outing, these things need to be considered. Though some of our activities will still be spontaneous ideas, many will benefit by advance planning. This preparation sheet will help us think about some of the things that need to be considered when planning a venture into the larger chickenyard.

1. What is our destination?

   _____

   _____

   _____

   _____

   _____

> *"Time heals griefs and quarrels, for we change and are no longer the same persons."*
>
> Pascal

7

7

2. How will we get there? *(This can actually be a great part of the adventure if an unusual method of transportation is chosen.)*

   - Walk
   - Blade
   - Ride Bikes
   - Drive

3. How many of us will be involved in this activity?
   Who is going?
   Does this activity allow all nest members who want to be involved to participate?
   What nest schedules need to be accommodated so all members can attend?

   _____

   _____

   _____

   _____

   _____

4. How much time will this activity take?

   _____

   _____

   _____

   _____

   _____

5. How much will this activity cost?

   _____

   _____

   _____

   _____

   _____

6. Are there any coupons in coupon books or papers that will help this event be economical?

_____

_____

_____

_____

_____

7. Is any special equipment needed?

_____

_____

_____

_____

_____

8. Will we need a meal before, after or during this event?
   Where will we eat?
   What's the cost?
   How long will it take to eat there?

_____

_____

_____

_____

_____

"Half our life is spent trying to find something to do with the time we have rushed through life trying to save."

Will Rogers

9. Will we eat out, eat in or take a meal with us from the nest?
   - If we take a meal with us:
   - What type of meal will best suit this activity and our method of transportation?
   - Who will prepare the meal?
   - Are any extra shopping duties required here?
   - What is the cost?

_____

_____

_____

_____

_____

10. How should we dress for this event?

_____
_____
_____
_____
_____

11. Where should we meet? *(This can also provide many interesting variations. Having a treasure hunt with clues to get to the point of meeting is one of our nest's favorite methods.)*

_____
_____
_____
_____
_____

12. Will other friendly nests or nest members be invited or is it just us?

_____
_____
_____
_____
_____

13. If other nests are invited, who will be paying? (Other nests can be given the activity sheets with all the information on it so they are prepared too.)

_____
_____
_____
_____

14. What is the exact date of our activity?

_____
_____
_____
_____
_____

"Both in thought and in feeling, even though time be real, to realise the unimportance of time is the gate of wisdom."

Bertrand Russell

15. What do we hope to accomplish with this activity? *(Check or circle all that apply.)*
    - Rest
    - Relaxation
    - Exercise
    - Fun
    - Being together
    - Learning
    - Worshiping

7

After the Nest Activity Preparation Worksheet is completed, the activity can be announced to the nest. Your creativity is the only limitation on how this announcement can be made.

You can write the announcement for a hike on a rock and place it in the middle of the kitchen table.

The announcement of a dinner of hamburgers at the local hamburger joint can be written on a hamburger wrapper, a bag from the place or a coke cup.

A movie can be announced by buying advance tickets and placing them in dinner plates at the table.

Anticipation for a surprise trip to a museum can be built by "artifact" clues that are left in a certain place each day, letting the nest place guesses for what the activity is going to be in an urn in the same location.

With nests having computers at their disposal, any number and type of "Nest Activity Invitations" can be devised and printed.

Planned nest activities can stimulate fun and creativity and at the same time teach how to plan in advance for success, fun and fulfillment.

> **"Time heals what reason cannot."**
> Seneca

A wonderful after-effect of good planning that shows real bonding is taking place and appreciation is being taught comes when nest members write thank yous, say thank yous or present some unusual form of thanks to the egg, chick or rooster who planned the activity.

But what about those nest members who are reluctant to participate in anything that has to do with this particular nest? What about those rotten eggs who are determined to bring this nest crashing to the ground by their hard-boiled attitudes?

Getting the Hard-Boiled Eggs Involved in Nest Activities

Even the most hard-boiled teenage egg will be a little curious as these planned activities begin. Even if the hard-boiled eggs in your nest do not agree to participate at first, when the rest of the nest is building excitement over the activity and the nestmates come back chirping wildly about the fun, the hard-boiled egg will begin to be curious. They ask short questions at first, then they begin to ask when the next activity will be and finally they ask if they will have a chance to plan one.

There are many options open to chicks and roosters when the hard-boiled egg threatens to turn rotten as a nest activity is announced. New nests may want to take a hard line and say, "As we begin these activities, everyone will be involved. Having fun together helps us get to know each other better. No egg will be allowed to let his rottenness spoil the activity for the nest. Any egg who chooses to be rotten will have kitchen duty for the next month." Any appropriate consequence can be named here.

The consequence should be named up front so that in the middle of the activity, when the rotten egg begins to stink, the chick or the rooster simply reminds the egg that he has just contracted for a month of kitchen duty. This reminder takes the place of long lectures, fractured eggs and freaked-out chicks and roosters. At this point in the activity, if the rotten egg needs to find a time-out place or to be entirely removed from the activity, there are several possible alternatives.

7

Rotten eggs can be sent back to the vehicle the nest traveled in. In some locations, rotten eggs can take public transportation back to the nest. Some areas will have a place that the rotten egg may "rest" until his rottenness no longer threatens to affect the welfare of the rest of the nest.

When a nest has an egg that frequently threatens to be rotten, symptoms of rotten behavior can and should be discussed before the activity. Describing the signs of rottenness gives one more reinforcing message that consequences will be administered if and when these signs are shown.

If the rotten egg seems bent on destroying nest fun, the next activity can simply be planned with the assumption that the rotten egg will not be involved. No nest squawking has to be done. Just quietly plan the activity assuming that this egg will not be involved. It can be planned when this egg is known to be busy. The activity sheets can come out with this egg's name missing.

When the rotten egg says (and believe me, the rotten egg will say this), "Why isn't my name on this list?" this egg can be told, "You want to go on this outing? That's great! We'll be happy to include you."

The rotten egg wants his stench to permeate the entire nest. When the nest finds a variety of air fresheners instead of reacting by noticing the stench and complaining about it, the rotten egg finds no pleasure in his rottenness. If no one notices that you stink, why bother?

> *"Come what come may, time and the hour run through the roughest day."*
>
> Shakespeare

Set Nest Guidelines for Schedule Planning

Some general guidelines for time planning will be helpful to you in the beginning, and a contract will make your desire to work together on this time project "real."

Begin by sharing some general success tips.

> *"Time is a kindly God."*
>
> Sophocles

7

Success Tips for Eggs About Personal Time Management

1. Prepare an a.m. and p.m. schedule to use each day.
   a. List daily morning activities.
   b. List daily evening activities.
   c. Estimate the time each activity takes.
   d. Ask the rooster or the chick to check these estimated times with you.
   e. Create an a.m. schedule by adding up your estimated times.
   f. Write down the time you must be ready in the morning.
   g. Subtract your estimated times from the time you have to be ready.
   h. Write down the time you must get up to be ready on time.
   i. Make a schedule starting with the time you have to get up.
   j. List each activity you have to do in the morning.
   k. Create the time you need to start each activity using your estimated times from letters A and D.
   l. Repeat letters E through K using evening activities and evening time estimates from letters B and D.
2. Keep an up-to-date daily, weekly or monthly planner.
3. Keep an organized school notebook.
4. Keep a daily to-do list that you prepare before roosting each night. Include things on your list like:
   a. "Hots"
   b. What to take to school
   c. What the chick and rooster need to know (remember bio- and stepchicks and roosters may each need to know these things)
      1. Do I need to be taken early for any before-school activities?
      2. Do I need to be picked up late for any after-school activities?
      3. Do I need extra money?
      4. Do I need lunch money?
      5. Is there a field trip or a permission slip?
   d. What do I need to take to day care?

5. Communicate with the chicks and roosters in your life.
   a. Tell your teachers if you have a question about class or an assignment.
   b. Tell your bio- and stepchicks and roosters if you have questions about school, friends, the nest, activities.
   c. Partner all chicks and roosters about your plans in advance of making them.
   d. Ask chicks and roosters if plans are OK before committing to them.
   e. Check coop finances before committing to plans with dollar amounts needed.
6. Set aside a "success hour" each night. Ask yourself:
   a. What nestwork do I have?
   b. What schoolwork do I have?
   c. Is there an extra-credit project I could work on?
   d. Is there something that needs to be done in the nest that I could volunteer to do?
   e. What do I want to learn more about?
      1. What could I read to learn more about this?
      2. What projects could help me learn more about this?
      3. What yard member could I talk to to learn more about this?
   f. What book(s) could I read for fun?
   g. What book(s) could I read for inspiration?
   h. What success tapes could I listen to?
   i. What story tapes could I listen to?
   j. What exercise could I do?
   k. What activity could I practice?
   l. What hobby could I do for fun?

7

"The lowest of jewelry thieves is the robber of that precious jewel of another's time."

Adlai Stevenson

Tips for young eggs:
Young eggs can be partnered in time management very early by:
1. *Asking them to help you lay out clothes for the morning.*
2. *Asking them to tell you what they need to do and you write the list.*
3. *Even before eggs can chirp, establishing a routine that you go through with them each morning in just the same way provides security and an early attitude of schedule adherence.*

> *"Our costliest expenditure is time."*
>
> Theophrastus

7

Time-Management Success Tips for Chicks and Roosters Who Are Helping Eggs

1. Project follow-up and follow-through is essential to your egg's success.

2. Provide positive feedback about egg's successful time management.

3. Provide coaching when the egg falters in time management.

4. Provide feedback by pointing out areas of improvement and brainstorming with the egg about solutions.

5. Supervise the "success hour" each night before roosting.

   A. Ask questions about schoolwork.

   B. Make certain you get the correct answer.

   C. Provide suggestions about how to use the hour.

   D. Suggest nestwork that could be done to help.

   E. When possible, work with eggs on library and reading projects.

   F. Model good reading and research habits.

   G. Provide magazine subscriptions.

   H. Provide in-nest helps as possible such as:

      1. Computer linkages and availability
      2. Encyclopedias and other reference materials
      3. Magazine subscriptions
      4. Necessary office materials and equipment

6. Provide a working model of successful time management in your own life.

After going over the Egg Success Tips together, prepare a Time Agreement.

Agreement for Personal Time Management

Part A: Egg Agreement

Because I am a part of my nest, I realize that my personal time management affects others.

I will manage my time responsibly and respectfully.

Name _____

Date _____

• • •

Part B: Chick and Rooster Agreement

Because I am a caring chick or rooster in your life, I realize that I need to help you with personal time management.

I will provide you with training and support in learning this valuable life skill.

I will manage my time to assist you in managing your time.

Name _____

Name _____

Date _____

Here is what an actual schedule created from the Success Tips format might look like.

Egg's A.M. Schedule

1.	Wake up		6:00 a.m.
2.	Take a shower	Six minutes	6:06 a.m.
3.	Get dressed	Ten minutes	6:16 a.m.
4.	Get hair fixed	Ten minutes	6:26 a.m.
5.	Eat breakfast	Twenty minutes	6:46 a.m.
6.	Brush teeth	Three minutes	6:49 a.m.
7.	Make bed	Three minutes	6:52 a.m.
8.	Check school bag	Five minutes	6:57 a.m.

(To make certain that everything I need is in my school bag, I will make a list the night before of everything I need. I will use this list to check off all the material I need in my bag.)

9. Get to van by 7:00 a.m.
(What are some chores I can do to help the nest if I am finished with my schedule earlier than I expect?)

"It takes a very long time to become young."

Pablo Picasso

Egg's P.M. Schedule

1. Put backpack in room One minute

2. Change to PJs or
   comfy clothes   Seven   minutes

3. Make lunch   Seven minutes

4. Study hour   Sixty minutes
   *(If there is no homework or if homework is finished, this
   time may be used for reading, crafts or projects.)*

5. Eat dinner with nest   Thirty minutes

6. Brush teeth   Six minutes
   *(This is the time when I really concentrate on brushing
   carefully and flossing.)*

7. During most evenings
   I will be able to have
   one hour of free time Sixty minutes

8. Story time with nest   Eighteen minutes

9. Go to bed   Six minutes
   (My bedtime is 9:00 p.m. I will adjust my free time to
   be certain that I am roosting, covers pulled up and snoring
   by that time.)

> *"Each moment is a place you've never been."*
>
> Mark Strand

Exercise: Prepare a.m. and p.m. schedules for each member
of the nest using the examples given as models and re-reading
the Egg, Chick and Rooster Success Tips.

Following are some blank sheets with top headings to help
give you a start. Copy these sheets for each nest member, read
the "tips" over together, look at the examples and try your own.

Egg A.M. Schedule

Name _____

Date _____

Activity	# of Minutes/Hours It Will Take	Time to Begin
_____	_____	_____
_____	_____	_____
_____	_____	_____
_____	_____	_____
_____	_____	_____
_____	_____	_____
_____	_____	_____
_____	_____	_____
_____	_____	_____
_____	_____	_____
_____	_____	_____
_____	_____	_____
_____	_____	_____

7

Egg P.M. Schedule

Name _____

Date _____

Activity	# of Minutes/Hours It Will Take	Time to Begin
_____	_____	_____
_____	_____	_____
_____	_____	_____
_____	_____	_____
_____	_____	_____
_____	_____	_____
_____	_____	_____
_____	_____	_____
_____	_____	_____
_____	_____	_____
_____	_____	_____
_____	_____	_____
_____	_____	_____

7

Chick A.M. Schedule

Name _____

Date _____

Activity	# of Minutes/Hours It Will Take	Time to Begin
_____	_____	_____
_____	_____	_____
_____	_____	_____
_____	_____	_____
_____	_____	_____
_____	_____	_____
_____	_____	_____
_____	_____	_____
_____	_____	_____
_____	_____	_____
_____	_____	_____
_____	_____	_____
_____	_____	_____
_____	_____	_____

7

Chick P.M. Schedule

Name _____

Date _____

Activity	# of Minutes/Hours It Will Take	Time to Begin
_____	_____	_____
_____	_____	_____
_____	_____	_____
_____	_____	_____
_____	_____	_____
_____	_____	_____
_____	_____	_____
_____	_____	_____
_____	_____	_____
_____	_____	_____
_____	_____	_____
_____	_____	_____
_____	_____	_____

7

Rooster A.M. Schedule

Name _____

Date _____

Activity	# of Minutes/Hours It Will Take	Time to Begin
_____	_____	_____
_____	_____	_____
_____	_____	_____
_____	_____	_____
_____	_____	_____
_____	_____	_____
_____	_____	_____
_____	_____	_____
_____	_____	_____
_____	_____	_____
_____	_____	_____
_____	_____	_____
_____	_____	_____
_____	_____	_____

7

Rooster P.M. Schedule

Name _____

Date _____

Activity	# of Minutes/Hours It Will Take	Time to Begin
_____	_____	_____
_____	_____	_____
_____	_____	_____
_____	_____	_____
_____	_____	_____
_____	_____	_____
_____	_____	_____
_____	_____	_____
_____	_____	_____
_____	_____	_____
_____	_____	_____
_____	_____	_____
_____	_____	_____

7

Job Descriptions Increase Positive Nest Management

Coming from different nests, we have different meanings attached to statements such as, "Clean your part of the nest." An egg is sent off to "clean your corner of the nest" and is quiet for a very long time. The chick or rooster who sent him is feeling quite satisfied that the job is being done according to the job description in the mind of the chick or rooster. This chicken who assigned the job has no doubt that he and the egg are on the same nest frequency about this task.

The chick or rooster goes to check on the egg only to find him seated in the middle of his corner of the nest playing with recently rediscovered Legos. You get this egg back on track, and he comes to you 30 minutes later and says he is ready for inspection. Nothing has been dusted, furniture has not been moved while vacuuming and it is still a pit by your definition.

Some chicks or roosters who say, "Clean your corner of the nest mean, "Straighten up your corner." Other chicks and roosters mean, "Start with cleaning those drawers, and don't stop until the carpet is swept, each item is dusted and your closet looks like the racks in a high-end retail clothing store."

To be certain that you are using similar definitions for nest jobs, job descriptions are a great communication tool. These job descriptions ...

1. Improve communication
2. Decrease stress
3. Decrease conflict

It was exactly this kind of definitional situation that sent Ross and me to the computer to negotiate "Room Cleaning Guidelines." Here's what ours look like.

Room Cleaning Guidelines

I. Put all clothes away neatly.

   A. All clothes need to be put neatly in drawers.
1. Underwear drawer
2. T-shirt drawer
3. Sock drawer
4. Jeans drawer
5. Sweaters/sweats drawer
6. Toy drawer

   B. Organize closet.
1. Hang all shirts together.
2. Hang all pants together.
3. Hang all jackets together.
4. Organize shoes.
5. Organize dirty-clothes baskets.

   C. Organize top of dresser neatly.
1. Remove all items from top of dresser
2. Dust dresser with cloth and dusting compound.
3. Dust items on dresser top before replacing them.
4. Arrange items neatly on dresser top for convenience of use.

   D. Organize area under bed.
1. Put toys in box.
2. Put all books on the shelf.
3. Replace all shoes in closet.

   E. Vacuum floor.
1. Move items on floor to get all dust bunnies.
2. Replace moved items.

   F. Change bedclothes and remake bed.

   G. Call Dad or Ruth-Ann to check cleaning according to guidelines.

II. Estimated time to accomplish this cleaning is two and one half hours.

   A. Set timer.

   B. Check at end of cleaning to see how much time it really took.

   C. Keep track of cleaning time for about three times, and then make a decision about how long cleaning actually takes.

> *"The expert in anything was once a beginner."*
>
> Anonymous

7

> *"The ability to beat the odds lies within us all."*
>
> Anonymous

7

Why "negotiate" guidelines? Why can't the chick or rooster just sit down separately or together and make up guidelines and hand them to the egg(s)? It's called "ownership." Eggs are much more agreeable about doing what they have planned and participated in themselves. The negotiated job description, laminated and placed in a position of prominence in the room, serves as a reminder to the egg that this is a nest chore.

This same description serves as a great checklist when the chick or rooster returns for checking the job. When you make these job descriptions one by one, you find that you soon have a Nest Operations Manual. When each job description is kept in the part of the nest where it is used, it serves as an empowerer, a reminder and a follow-through tool.

It empowers eggs, chicks or roosters who have not done this job in a while. They do not have to go ask any other nest member, "How do you do this?" It reminds the entire nest that this job needs to be done. Because of this reminder, it serves as a follow-through tool and a reminder to older members of the nest to check to see that this job is being done regularly.

The main benefit of this job-description tool is that it creates an environment of fairness. When every nest member who ever does this job is required to do it using the same rules, it helps the job requirements to be viewed as fair. The evaluation is also fair because the same list is used for each nest performer.

What about activities during those long summer vacations in the nest?

Successfully Sweating Out the Summer in the Nest

Summer vacations in the nest can be extremely successful. If you do not plan for these vacation times you are begging for nest destruction. Since for many stepnests this is the only extended period of time together, many negative things can happen without planning.

Some biochicks and roosters in the stepnest feel that since this is the only significant amount of time spent together in this stepnest, this should be one long recreation period for the eggs.

130

Chores should be light to none at all, and as much time as possible should be spent having fun. This usually causes stepchicks and roosters to squawk loudly about things like teaching egg responsibility and "How are these eggs going to learn skills for hatching?"

The only way for summers to work in the nest is for them to be organized. Eggs need and like structure. They like for their crates to be orderly. Not knowing exactly how to accomplish this themselves, they look to step- and biochicks and roosters to provide this structure. If they do not find it, they may end up looking like "Humpty Dumpty" (a not-so-successful egg from literature).

This summer we agreed that in our nest, we each wanted to spend time learning and making certain that good study skills gained during the school year were not lost. That's how the "Ross/Cam Summer List of To-Do's" began. You can see that it expanded as we got inspired while creating it. We partnered to create it with eggs, chick and rooster chirping in from time to time.

It served as a great impetus for summer growth and was a wonderful checklist to communicate about and use as an evaluation tool at the end of each week.

> *"It's not the hours you put in; it's what you put in the hours."*
>
> Elmer Leterman

Summer List of "To-Do's"

Tape Programs:

1. Listen to two full audiocassette tape programs before school starts.
2. Budget 30 minutes of 24 days of July or August to listen.
3. Each side takes about 30 minutes.
4. Discuss ideas from each tape side with Dad or R-A.
    A. Tell us one thing you learned from that side.
    B. Tell us one action you will take because of listening to that side of the tape

7

> *"Who dares noth-*
> *ing, need hope for*
> *nothing."*
>
> Schiller

Books:

1. Read one book every two weeks.
2. Make oral or written report to turn in to Dad or R-A.
3. Books must be BOOKS, not magazines, and must be okayed by Dad or R-A., or the Librarian will help you find a good book.
4. One of the books should be about study skills to help you for next year.
5. Books about and by successful people would be great books to read.

Prepare Your School Goals for Next Year

1. School goals need to be typed on the computer, printed out, three-hole punched and put in the front of next year's school notebook.
2. One copy of your school goals should be on the wall of your room.
3. Each goal should have three action steps which will help you meet the goal.

Budget Goals and Responsibilities

1. Ten percent of all money received whether by gift or by earning goes to the church.
2. Ten percent of all money received goes into savings.
3. Ten percent of all money received goes into a mutual fund.
4. Seventy percent of all money received is to be budgeted by you for expenses in the need, want, gift categories.
5. See Dad or R-A for budget approval.
6. Keep appropriate expense, budget and savings records.

Household Chores to Negotiate

1. Water plants.
2. Animal duties:

A. Feed and water
B. Medicine
C. Litter box
3. Vacuuming upstairs and downstairs
4. Restrooms cleaning and supplies
5. Laundry and supplies
6. Household cleaning supplies inventory
7. Grocery-list items
    A. Favorite foods
    B. Foods you took the last of
8. Trash
9. Clock winding
10. Outside chores:
    A. Edging
    B. Mowing
    C. Weeding
    D. Policing the outdoor area
11. Room care and cleaning
12. Athletic preparation and packing
13. Packing for biochick's house
14. Others as needed

General Rules for Jobs:

1. Prepare a written job description for each job.
    A. List all of the steps needed to begin, process and complete the job.
    B. Job descriptions should be approved by Dad or R-A.
    C. Job descriptions should be posted close to where the job will be done.
2. All jobs must be inspected before other activities are begun.
3. Finishing jobs is a focus.
4. Not waiting to be asked is a focus.

The eggs felt really good about a productive, fun summer and were ready for school to begin. This list, negotiated together, lets them feel in control of their own lives even when doing things they might not freely choose to do.

"Not the cry, but the flight of the wild duck, leads the flock to fly and follow."

Chinese Proverb

7

Don't Get Caught in the Chickenwire at Nest Project Times

It takes a lot of fancy footwork for most nests to keep from getting caught in the chickenwire when it's time for nest projects. Few eggs, chicks or roosters really crow with anticipation about such necessary nest maintenance as yard work, garage cleaning, basement organization or nestpainting and nestkeeping.

In our nest, we have found that project times can be more fun and less scratchy when we know what is expected up front, we negotiate expectations and actual work loads, plan some fun into the project, know there will be an end to the project, and realize the "big picture" purpose of the project. We developed the "How to Manage Nest Project Time" worksheet. Here it is.

How to Manage Nest Project Time

Planning ahead and being aware of what we need to successfully complete jobs will eliminate much of the unpleasantness, squawking and general upset in the coop that happens when our nest needs to do a project.

1. What is the project that needs to be done?

    _____
    _____
    _____
    _____
    _____

2. How long will it take?

    A. When will we start?

    _____
    _____
    _____
    _____
    _____

B. When do we expect to be finished?

_____

_____

_____

_____

_____

3. What materials are needed? Prepare a checklist after asking and checking to see:

A. Do we have the materials now?

_____

_____

_____

_____

_____

B. Where are they?

_____

_____

_____

_____

_____

C. What materials need to be borrowed?

_____

_____

_____

_____

_____

D. What materials need to be purchased?

_____

_____

_____

_____

_____

E. Where will we store them when we are finished?

_____
_____
_____
_____
_____

4. What could we do that will make this work more enjoyable?

A. Someone to work with?

_____
_____
_____
_____
_____

B. A cold drink?

_____
_____
_____
_____
_____

C. Some music?

_____
_____
_____
_____
_____

D. Your suggestions

_____
_____
_____
_____
_____

7

5. What are the nest benefits of doing this job?

   A. A better looking nest?
   B. A yard we are proud of?
   C. A more pleasant nest environment?

   _____

   _____

   _____

   _____

   _____

6. What are the personal benefits to doing this job?

   A. Self-satisfaction?
   B. Self-esteem?
   C. Learning?
   D. Helping?

   _____

   _____

   _____

   _____

   _____

7. What are the consequences of not doing the job properly,
   not doing the job at all, not completing the job or having
   to be pushed to complete the job?

   A. Unpleasant squawking?
   B. Not having the warm feeling of, "Look what I did!"
   C. Punishment/consequences?
   D. Causing another nest member to squawk?
   E. A nest environment that is an embarrassment?

   _____

   _____

   _____

   _____

   _____

7

Great organization helps you to be successful doing projects that improve the nest. Pride in the nest helps each member to feel better about being in this nest. When you work to make the nest a pleasant place, you begin to feel ownership in this nest. When you own a piece of the nest, you begin to care about this nest and its inhabitants.

Are there any other "nestcessities" that you can organize, plan or be proactive about that turn potential disaster into outstanding success?

Don't Fight Over the Grain and Seedlings

"Remember that the faith that moves mountains always carries a pick."

Anonymous

Coming from different nests, you have developed a taste for your own specific types and brands of grains. You like your seedlings cooked just a certain way. You tend to be suspicious of any new types of grains or seedlings which are prepared in a way you have never seen them prepared before.

In settling into this new nest, you will find that food can be a major source of stress and conflict. Eggs tell the chick, "I don't like that!" after the chick has spent hours planning a special meal and cooking it carefully. The chick has really invested time in preparing this meal just to suit these eggs. Then the ungrateful eggs refuse to eat. The chick invests more time in the next meal she fixes, with the same result. Even when she has consulted the eggs about what they want to eat and how they want it prepared, comments such as "My biomom does it better than this" just cause severe cases of ruffled chick feathers.

It is usually at this point that the rooster gets into the squawking. He either tells the eggs to, "Eat it and like it," or he suggests to the chick that she fix something else. Either way, the entire nest loses.

It's a good idea to make food lists in the earliest stages of your nest-building. When favorite grains are written down, it helps keep eggs from shifting stories in the middle of a meal. Some eggs find it really amusing to say, "This is my favorite grain," and then when the chick fixes it say, "I don't like this." When the chick says, "You said this was your favorite," the egg replies, "No, I didn't." Now there is serious nest warfare. The egg chuckles as yet another battle begins, usually between the chick and the rooster. The egg has accomplished his mission of creating disharmony at feeding time.

When meal choices are written down, several benefits occur:

1. The choices are in writing for all to see and approve.

2. Written choices allow advance shopping and planning.

3. Written choices help nestmates to get to know each other better.

4. Written choices allow surprises and special celebration meals.

When you work on feeding time together, incorporating in to this work respectful ways to express yourself about types of grains you really don't like, you'll find mealtimes to be fun times rather than fight times.

Begin with the preferred-grains worksheet.

Preferred-Grains Worksheet

1. My favorite breakfast meal is ...

   _____

   _____

   _____

2. My favorite lunch meal is ...

   _____

   _____

   _____

3. My favorite dinner is ...

   _____

   _____

   _____

4. My favorite main dish is ...

_____

_____

_____

5. My favorite dessert is ...

_____

_____

_____

6. My favorite vegetable is ...

_____

_____

_____

7. My favorite salad and salad dressing is ...

_____

_____

_____

8. My favorite cereals are ...

_____

_____

_____

9. My favorite soup is ...

_____

_____

_____

10. My favorite snacks are ...

_____

_____

_____

7

11. My favorite drinks are ...

_____
_____
_____

12. I like to ...

☐ Buy my lunch at school/work
☐ Take my lunch from the nest to school/work

7

Another very empowering and freeing tactic for the nest is for chick and rooster to teach the eggs to prepare their own sack lunches for school. You teach about food groups and healthy lunches. Then you go together to shop for items that will stay in stock. Eggs can even be given a budget and be allowed to go solo in the store to find and purchase their own lunch items.

Waste and lunches returned uneaten go down drastically when eggs have a say in and responsibility for their own lunches. It is also wise to teach eggs to prepare breakfasts, lunches and parts of dinner when eating in the nest. At different ages and with different interest levels, eggs are taught at an early stage to be independent in matters of feeding times.

Some real nest bonding can occur when special feeding times such as holiday and celebration meals are planned for. Using the china and cloth napkins and candles to create a special setting can bring a nest to greater unity. Even having a special dress code can help. It is really exciting to work together to prepare a special meal, then separate to clean up and change and come back to share the meal together.

Eating meals together can be a real de-stressor. Are there any other ways to decrease stress in the nest?

> *"Chance sometimes opens the door, but luck belongs to the good players."*
>
> Bernard Bruch

Avoid Petty Pecking in the Nest to Decrease Nest Stress

It seems that after just a brief time spent in the nest together, you find just what it takes to make each egg crack, causes the chick to squawk and roasts the rooster. Then you spend time planning to push exactly the right buttons that causes each of these things to happen.

Learning what causes stress for each member of the nest and really working to avoid stress-producing situations can lead to healthier, happier nestmates. Research shows that the time of life from age 15 to age 30 is one of the peak periods for stress-related illness.

To know how to manage stress, you have to do three things:

1. Increase your knowledge about what stresses each nestmate out.

2. Discover your own hot buttons.

3. Try out new no-pecking behaviors.

To accomplish these three objectives, use the "De-stressed Nest Worksheet."

The De-Stressed Nest Worksheet

1. What nest situations cause stress for me?

   _____

   _____

   _____

   _____

   _____

2. What nestmates peck at me most?

   _____

   _____

   _____

   _____

   _____

3. What types of pecking fry me most? What are my "hot buttons"?

   _____

   _____

   _____

   _____

   _____

4. What pecking causes me to jump out of the nest?

   _____

   _____

   _____

   _____

   _____

5. What type of pecking causes me to want to push a nestmate out of the nest?

   _____

   _____

   _____

   _____

   _____

7

6. In the past, when a nestmate has pushed one of my "hot buttons," I have ...

7. In the future, when a nestmate pushes one of my "hot buttons," I will ...

   A. Give myself permission to pause before pecking back
   B. Realize that I can choose not to peck back at all
   C. Know that I can say, "We need to talk about what just happened in this nest. Let's do it later when each of us has had time to think."
   D. Say, "That comment just pushed my hot button. It hurt my feelings and made me angry. In the future, please speak to me with respect."
                          or ...
      "What just happened here really pushed one of my hot buttons. In the future please..." *(explain the behavior you think is fair and respectful behavior).*

> *"Kindness can become its own motive. We are made kind by being kind."*
>
> Eric Hoffer

Knowing how to manage stress can improve how you feel about yourself and how you relate to each other. You can be proud of your ability to choose and be in control, instead of reacting and lashing out.

De-Stress the Nest Summary

In our nest, we try to make everything we do fun and training for life skills. Your nest will be happier as you each decrease individual and group stress through the accomplishment that time management brings.

You will discover that especially with hectic nest styles that are exacerbated by the complicated time schedules of a stepnest, it is important to increase productivity and reduce stress through time management, and that takes careful planning.

Have a great time using the tools in this chapter to live sunny-side-up!

CHAPTER 8

Communicate with Constructive Clucking

"When were you planning on telling me about this?"

"All that is necessary to break the spell of inertia and frustration is this: Act as if it were impossible to fail."

Dorothea Brande

Plan Before Clucking

Do you ever plan what you are going to say before you say it? You would not attempt to build a chicken coop without elaborate plans, but here you are trying to build nests and hatch eggs without even a sketch of what to say and how to say it, much less what you'd like each of you to do, think or feel at the end of this conversation. Wouldn't "outcome-based communication" be a better idea?

Why not begin with a plan and a direction instead of rushing ahead and sticking both chickenfeet in your beak? I know a lot about rushing ahead, and I'm fairly familiar with the taste of my feet.

Just a few months into our marriage, Steve and I decided to give our first dinner party. We had divided responsibilities to achieve teamwork (and mostly to get jobs done faster). One of Steve's responsibilities was to light the barbecue grill.

Our guests were to arrive at 6:00 p.m. We were going to eat early because other activities were planned for later. I assumed

8

that the grill would be lit by around 5:30 p.m. I checked about that time and there was no action in that area of the deck. I also assumed that Steve would be with me at the front door greeting guests.

The first guests arrived at 6:02. Where was Steve? I greeted them, seated them and got them something to drink. I then went on a hunt for that man. I found him cheerfully stepping out of the shower, whistling! Beyond furious I said, "Steve, in what century did you plan to light the barbecue grill?" The whistling stopped abruptly, his face turned red, and he went into orbit verbally, emotionally and physically.

When he finally touched down, I said, "I understand that wasn't the nicest thing to say to you, but what made you so angry?" He replied, "You used your teacher voice." I immediately sat down on the bed and said, "You know, I think you're right."

I wasn't even aware that I had a teacher voice. I'm certain after 17 years of teaching that my "teacher voice" was well developed. It just had never been called to my attention before. I was running a couple of work scenarios from the last few weeks through my mind as I sat on that bed. I had been dissecting a difficult situation with a couple of colleagues trying to discover WHAT I had said that had caused an angry reaction. Now I realized it wasn't WHAT I said, it was HOW I said it. Interesting that with two degrees in communication, I was just now figuring this out! Chicks and roosters don't like teacher voices; eggs really hate them.

Ever had a situation like this in your nest? These communication breakdowns typically occur due to:

1. Not planning before clucking

2. Filters that create piles of "stuff" in the message

3. Lack of awareness of what the other poultry is really hearing when you're clucking

4. Failure to set nest ground rules

I decided our nest, starting with me, needed to plan before clucking. Have your nest try the Constructive Clucking Planning Sheet.

Constructive Clucking Planning Sheet

1. What do I hope will happen as a result of this conversation?

   _____
   _____
   _____
   _____
   _____

2. How will each person in the conversation benefit as a result of this conversation?

   _____
   _____
   _____
   _____
   _____

8

3. What do I have to lose if this conversation doesn't go well?

   _____
   _____
   _____
   _____
   _____

4. What filters might cause the other person(s) in this conversation to hear something differently than I want him/her to?

   _____
   _____
   _____
   _____
   _____

> *"Half the world is composed of people who have something to say and can't, and the other half who have nothing to say and keep on saying it."*
>
> Robert Frost

5. How should I sound to get the most benefit for both of us from this conversation?

_____

_____

_____

_____

_____

6. What body language do I need to be careful of in this conversation?

_____

_____

_____

_____

8

Filters That Create Piles of "Stuff"

Communication is a tricky game in the best of nests. Many times you are not aware of how the message is actually getting across. Communication is even tougher in the stepnest, where there are more filters working to prevent the message from getting through the way you intend. Each of you are listening and talking through barriers that create greater misunderstandings.

What are some of the filters that distort messages for nestmates? What are some filters that distort messages from the chick and rooster, eggs and the yard?

Chicks and roosters filter based on what happened in the last nest. If the first chick or rooster was a controller, the new chick or rooster is suspected and convicted because she suggests how to schedule an evening. A chick or rooster spends too long on the phone with the exchick or rooster and his voice sounds too friendly, and the new chick suspects that the past nest relationship is not really over.

Eggs filter and worry that this relationship between the chick and rooster might not last either. They filter and feel guilty for enjoying the new stepchick and in the middle of a satisfying experience, find reasons to be unpleasant to relieve their guilt.

Filters are part of each nestmate's history that cause you to hear squawking when chirping was intended. Filters also cause nestmates to "hear" intonations and body language differently than the sender intended. No two of you have exactly the same history, so some things that would not offend you offend the other person.

For example, it really ruffles my feathers for someone to say, "You look like a real family." Well, what are we if not real? Phantom chickens? It makes me crazy to hear this because I feel that it degrades us or makes us second class to have this comment made. That same comment, made in that same way to another person, might not have the same interpretation.

There are a number of filters that affect each of you. Here are a few examples.

- Steve, at first, did not like to use the word "step" anything.

- I don't like having anyone say, "You're not the mother."

- Cam can't stand to hear, "You're too short to play first base."

- Ross feels upset when he perceives that anyone is trying to boss him around.

- Stephanie reacts fairly violently to being called a boy.

What are some of the filters that exist in your nest? Use the "Stuff" Meter to find out.

> *"You can have brilliant ideas, but if you can't get them across, your ideas won't get you anywhere."*
>
> Lee Iacocca

8

The "Stuff" Meter

1. Things nestmates say to me that really bug me:

    _____
    _____
    _____
    _____

2. How do these things make you feel?

_____
_____
_____
_____

3. How do you react when you hear this?

_____
_____
_____
_____

4. What things do nestmates do that really push your buttons?

_____
_____
_____
_____

5. How do these things make you feel?

_____
_____
_____
_____

6. How do you react when nestmates do these things?

_____
_____
_____
_____

Sharing the information on your "Stuff" Meter is risky because others can use this information to push your buttons even more times. There are two reasons for sharing this information. It causes you to think about your "stuff" and realize what is happening to you when someone says or does something that just instantly causes you to be angry. Sharing the "Stuff" Meter with others allows you to begin or continue to build a climate of respect in the nest by working to avoid "stuff."

In your communication, you have to keep reminding yourself that it doesn't matter what you think you said. What matters is what they heard.

How Clucking Can Sound Like Squawking

"Only seven percent of the actual message comes through the words."

Ruth-Ann Clurman

You are often unaware of what the nest is hearing when you cluck. You mistakenly think that your clucking is the biggest part of the message when, in reality, words are the smallest piece of the communication pie. Only seven percent of the actual message comes through the words. Thirty-eight percent comes through tone of voice. Fifty-five percent of the message comes from body language.

So what's wrong with this nest? Why don't they correctly interpret my clucking?

Have you ever said to one of your eggs, "Don't take that tone with me?" It wasn't the egg's words but tone of voice the egg used that ruffled your feathers.

In our nest, we have recently gone through this battle with the word "fine." "Fine" sounds like a perfectly good word until Ross says it after I say, "You need to be back from your bike ride in one hour," and "fine" comes back from the Ross-Egg in a very tense, sassy squawk. At this point my response is, "Don't ever say 'fine' to me again!" Sound familiar?

Try using the Squawk Meter with your nest to open communication on this subject.

The Squawk Meter

1. What tone of voice can nestmates use that just rocks your roost?

   _____

   _____

   _____

   _____

2. How do you feel when you hear this tone?

_____

_____

_____

_____

3. Who uses this tone most often?

_____

_____

_____

_____

4. What tone of voice would you be more comfortable with?

_____

_____

_____

_____

Tone of voice also is impacted by **when** it is used. A semi-sarcastic tone can be used when you are having fun and joking. If the same tone is used when you are disagreeing, it can have a totally different effect.

Who uses the tone of voice makes a difference too. The chick or rooster can use a tone of voice with an egg that suggests authority and she doesn't resent it, but let another egg use that tone and you'd think the sky is falling!

Certain Types of Strutting Can Be Really Annoying

Some poultry really get irritating with the way they strut, stare and fluff their feathers. Body language in the nest can speak volumes, and many of them are not pleasant reading. Some eggs are really great at stomping off and slamming doors when life in the nest doesn't seem to be going their way. Other eggs can give a "look" that singes your feathers.

"If people around you will not hear you, fall down before them and beg their forgiveness, for in truth you are to blame."

Fyodor
Dostoyevsky

8

What about the egg who breaks eye contact when you are talking to him about an important issue. You say, "Look at me when I am talking to you," as you remember your own biochick taking your chin in her not-so-gentle-at-the-moment wingtip, turning you to face her and saying the same words you now hear yourself saying to this stepegg.

What kind of body language used by other nest members really upsets you or singes your feathers?

The Sickening Strut Meter

1. Which nestmate's body language makes you feel angry?

   _____

   _____

   _____

   _____

2. What is it about this "strut" that bugs you?

   _____

   _____

   _____

   _____

3. What body language could this nestmate use that would be less annoying?

   _____

   _____

   _____

   _____

Now that you have completed the "Stuff" Meter, the Squawk Meter and the Sickening Strut Meter, you are ready to complete the Stuff Avoidance Agreement. This will help you take the things you have learned that really bug you about your nestmates' behavior and turn these negatives into positives.

Each nestmate who appeared as a name on any of the meters should fill out a Stuff Avoidance agreement with each nestmate affected negatively by his/her words or actions.

Stuff Avoidance Agreement

Dear _____,

I understand that these things I say,
(List the things on the nestmate's Stuff Meter)

and these things I do,
(List the things on the nestmate's Stuff Meter)

really bug you.

Now that I know what I say and do that causes you to feel you are stepping in "stuff," I will not say or do these things.

Sincerely,

_____
(Name of "stuffer")

> *"A leading marriage counselor says that at least half of the divorces in this country can be traced to faulty communication between spouses."*
>
> Anonymous

Constructive Clucking Is a Tough Goal

Honest communication seems to be tougher in stepnests. There is a tendency for biochicks and roosters who have issues and agendas of their own to knowingly and unknowingly misrepresent the truth to each other. Sometimes the eggs even become part of this dishonesty. A biochick may say, "Now don't tell your dad this but ... " How can we expect eggs to know telling the truth is an important value and to communicate openly if partial truth or untruth is consistently modeled for them?

Ground rules for communicating chick to rooster and chick and rooster to eggs are needed. As a stepchick or rooster, you may walk into a very dysfunctional communication situation. You observe that the individuals most often caught in this trap are the eggs. It may seem to you that they are often being used as carrier pigeons to deliver messages. The biochick says to the eggs, "Tell your dad that..." Then, if messages are not delivered or are delivered incorrectly, guess who gets squawked at?

When this happens, the rooster needs to have a conversation where he sits down with the eggs and the exchick and explains that the eggs are not to carry messages anymore. If the chick or rooster want to communicate with each other, they need to do it directly.

At the same time, rules need to be set for separating from the former nest. Sometimes the expoultry seem to be communicating too much. Many stepchicks and roosters that I speak with complain that the exchick or rooster calls four and five times a day to "confer." The conferences never seem to be over consequential matters. They are an attempt to continue the ties of the former nest.

Some chicks and roosters have not closed the door on their last nest. Chicks and roosters who have this lack of closure:

- Should not try to continue the former nest relationship.

- Should not enjoy attempt to bomb the new nest with fertilizer.

- Should not use the eggs as an excuse to try to continue their past nest relationship with the other chick or rooster.

This raises the legitimate question, "If you wanted to communicate this much, why did you get a divorce?"

Willingness to speak up and set ground rules about frequency of communication can save disappointment and trouble later. When you are truly uncomfortable about continued communication with the previous nest, you need to squawk. Then rules can be established about frequency and type of communication. For example:

1. Except in an emergency, calls will not be made to the former nest.

2. Communication by means of a note or a letter periodically can establish time-scheduling issues.

Many stepchicks and roosters feel that calls made from the former nest are an orchestrated attempt to produce an intended disruption and cause trouble in the new nest.

> *"Personally I'm always ready to learn, although I do not always like being taught."*
>
> Winston Churchill

8

> *"Grownups never understand any thing by themselves, and it is tiresome for children to be always and forever explaining things to them."*
>
> Antoine de St. Exupery

8

You can't avoid all unpleasantness and misunderstanding, but not to address issues in advance or as they appear simply causes chicks and roosters to carry around resentments. The filters multiply, and more communication is broken because we have added these resentments to the ones already there. The situation becomes impossible if issues go unaddressed. The chickenyard becomes laden with stones to step over, whole coops to step around, lots of "stuff" to step in, chickens with ruffled feathers to avoid and, most importantly, crushed eggs.

A stepchick or rooster walks into an operating chicken coop. If no attempt has been made to organize the coop's communication efforts or if attempts have been made and the system is broken, make new rules. Each nester in the newly reorganized coop should partner in the rule making and be aware of the importance of these rules.

Here is an example of rules that are important to a nest with open communication.

1. Eggs will be expected to be truthful.

2. Eggs will not be carrier pigeons.

3. Eggs have a right to ask for what they need or want.

4. Eggs have a right to know about information that affects their future.

5. Eggs have a right to know the truth.

6. Chicks and roosters will limit communication time with exes.

7. Exes will communicate without using current spouses as mediators.

8. The time and privacy of each nest will be respected.

9. Values of each nest will be acknowledged, especially when very different.

10. Honest communication will be a goal.

You may need other types of rules to deal with the subject of honesty itself. Eggs have a difficult time hatching and will crack before they hatch if they have to constantly wonder, "To whom may I say what, when?" or "Am I going to be grilled or fried when I go back to the other nest this time?" And, yes, this is all as confusing as it sounds!

Here are some examples of ideas eggs need to be comfortable with:

- It's OK to be confused.

- It's OK to say, "I'd rather be with you."

- It's OK to be angry with situations.

- You have a right to expect parenting from chicks and roosters.

- It's OK to ask for help.

"Not to dream boldly may turn out to be simply irresponsible."

George Leonard

8

The need that eggs have to talk openly about things that concern them, the need they have to have foods they like in the nest, the need to have some free time, the need to have rules — all these things must be discussed openly, and the atmosphere of freedom to express appropriately needs to be created.

Rules for difficult times need to be established, too. At times like weddings and graduations, you can say what a stepchick friend and mentor of mine says, "This is your event. You are the director. I am your support person. Here are the pieces that need to be dealt with. Here's what needs to be done. You tell me what, where and when. I'll be available as you see fit to ask me." These important, once-in-lifetime times should not be used as power struggles and "gotcha" opportunities.

Beware of the Manipulative Egg

Eggs learn very quickly how to manipulate the chickenyard. When they realize that communication is strained, they begin what my mom used to call, "Working both ends against the middle."

> *"Much unhappiness has come into the world because of bewilderment and things left unsaid."*
>
> Dostoyvsky

They then use the system to their advantage. This usually ends up causing terrible chaos in the chickenyard. At times like this, eggs need to be put in the scrambler.

Here's how the scrambler works. When Cameron was about nine, he was working on a science project for competition. He didn't really want to work on this project, so he told one story to his biochick and another to his biorooster. Each bioparent thought the other had the progress of the project under control. When Steve got down to really questioning him about his project, Steve found that no real progress was being made.

Cam managed to make it look to both parents as if the other was at fault. My long years of teaching and listening to kids pit parents against teachers began to come in handy, and I started to hear some flaws in the story. Because his biochick and Steve were now at serious odds with each other, the adults agreed that I would mediate a truth session where all combatants were present and required to confront each other with the truth.

Cam had managed to get both households in a complete uproar trying to get out of his science project. When we faced off with all persons present, he was caught cold in his manipulation. There are times when households really need to cooperate for the peace and sanity of the entire chickenyard. Eggs need to be aware that this kind of tactic is a dishonest communication move and will not be tolerated. Facing the scrambler makes this point quite clearly. We haven't had to use it since.

Communication with the Other Chick or Rooster

Communication understandings about how and whether "steps" and "bios" will communicate need to be determined. The eggs need to be filled in about what these understandings are. It isn't necessary for the two nests to meet together to determine these understandings. You can simply decide what type of communication you are comfortable with and explain to the eggs that this is how you will be proceeding.

It usually isn't even necessary for a stepchick or rooster to communicate directly with the other nest at all. When this communication is tense for whatever reason, it scrambles the eggs.

One of the first questions that Stephanie asked me was, "Is my mother your friend?" I wanted to say, "Are you kidding? Absolutely not!" That however, was too brutally honest. What I chose to say was, "A friend is someone you know very well and someone you pick to spend time with. I do not know your mother well at all. I have already chosen my friends with whom I spend time." I found that when ground rules about the relationship with the biochick or rooster are set down, the eggs are much more at ease and much happier.

When we first began attending events where all three parents were present, the tension for everyone was visible. The eggs, who liked me and had fun with me when their biochick was not present, didn't know if they should even talk to me when she was present. My filters began to say, "What's wrong with them that they ignore me when she's around? Don't they really like me?" I began avoiding events where I might be in this situation because these times were extremely painful. I began building dread in the pit of my stomach days in advance of these encounters.

Finally Steve said, "You can't avoid this forever. You've got to have enough belief in yourself and in the kids to show up and stand up for yourself."

I still couldn't buy the idea that we had to sit in the same area and pretend to be friendly. To me, this was false. My compromise move was that I would go to the events, but we would not have to sit together and pretend to be one big happy yard. We're not and never will be. There is too much negative history. Besides, eggs can see through this kind of falsehood, and it makes them uncomfortable. I also noticed that the eggs acted out in really unacceptable ways when two chicks and the rooster were present.

This caused another communication issue: "Who disciplines these guys when all three of us are present?" This issue becomes even more pronounced when different standards of discipline are operative and there is no coordination or standard setting between nests.

When we made this decision not to pretend, we told the eggs that it was uncomfortable for me to sit with their biochick. We told them it didn't matter where they chose to sit. Probably, they

> *"When the eyes say one thing, and the tongue another, a practised man relies on the language of the first."*
>
> Emerson

8

"Use what language you will, you can never say anything but what you are."

Emerson

would make different decisions at different times. We told them we would not have our feelings hurt no matter what choice they made.

The relaxation on the faces of the eggs at the next joint event was visible. They chatted freely with each nest and bounced back and forth with more freedom than ever before. Their acting out decreased dramatically. Chicks and roosters tend to feel that they have to put on a front with eggs. The eggs can see it, and what you are teaching them is to be false and manipulative.

The stepchick or rooster does not have to be involved in direct communication with the biochick or rooster. The type and kind of communication between the bio chick or rooster and the stepchick or rooster can run the gamut in the chickenyard from "friendly" to "we do not choose to communicate in any way." The type chosen will depend on the chicks and roosters involved, their comfort zones and their history.

In our situation, Steve and I decided that the biochick and rooster should be the ones in direct communication. I found myself listening to things I did not want to hear about my husband and feeling the need to defend him when I was asked to deliver a message or was given information to pass to him. I established the rule that I do not get involved in this interaction. I am not part of that dysfunctional relationship and do not choose to be included in it.

Other nests have made other types of arrangements that work for them. The key to success is having the freedom to make arrangements that work for each yard and making the ground rules known to all the chickens. Each chick or rooster in the coop should feel as comfortable as possible with the rules and be open about what works for him/her.

Nests can be successful without establishing relationships among or between chicks or roosters. The eggs receive false input if chicks and roosters pretend to be friends when they are not. It's also great training for eggs to realize that even when persons do not choose to be friends, they don't have to fight. We have used this to teach the concept that we can "agree to disagree" without being disagreeable.

Chicken-Scratching Can Work Before Clucking

> *"To think justly, we must understand what others mean: to know the value of our thoughts, we must try their effect on other minds."*
>
> William Hazlett

Have you ever been crying so hard you couldn't talk? When you tried to talk you were hiccuping so much you were unintelligible? Sometimes you are crying so hard inside that the hiccups are mental. You just can't look at the other person and even think much less talk.

At times like this, chicken-scratching helps. You can write notes to your chick or rooster, and you can write notes to the eggs. You can write to the biochick or rooster and she can write to you. It helps to be able to express what you really feel without involving the body-language and tone-of-voice factors which can escalate squawking and fighting.

When you write, it also helps you to look at what you have written and say, "Is this exactly what I mean?" You can review and rewrite, which you can't do when you speak. When you write, the person to whom you are writing has time to read and reread at her leisure and the opportunity to respond thoughtfully.

It is often easier to really express yourself when you write, whereas it is more difficult to be honest or assertive in person. The "I feel, here's why, here's what I think is fair" organization pattern discussed in the anger and resentment chapter is helpful to structure thoughts. For a brief review, here it is:

1. "I feel ... "

    _____

    _____

    _____

    _____

2. "Here's why ... "

    _____

    _____

    _____

    _____

3. "Here's what I think is fair ... "

_____

_____

_____

_____

Thinking and planning before you squawk can make a big difference in your peace of mind and in your fairness as you communicate.

Nest Meetings as a Communication Tool

We have found family meetings to be a constructive and effective way to communicate. The "Nest Meeting Success Tips" and the format which follow are ones that we use. I have also included the letter which invited our family to the first family meeting we had. The letter and the accompanying "documentation" about slip-ups plus the breakfast-meeting responsibilities were placed on each person's pillow the night before the meeting.

The "Because I Care About My Nest, I Will Be Responsible," worksheet was what we used in the nest meeting. The blank "Rules" sheets were what we developed and filled in as a result of the meeting.

Success Tips for Nest Meetings

1. The chick and rooster should discuss the plan of action.
2. Plan together what the meeting should accomplish.
3. Determine whether the whole nest needs to be there.
4. Stick to a few agenda items.
5. Try to deal with one topic per meeting.
6. Decide who will speak first and lay the groundwork.
7. Follow your agenda.
8. Gently remind those who get on other subjects that there will be other meetings.

> _"Good communication is stimulating as black coffee, and just as hard to sleep after."_
>
> Anne Morrow Lindbergh

9. Time speakers so that:
   - A. Each egg, chick or rooster gets to speak.
   - B. One speaker doesn't monopolize the whole time.
   - C. Attention spans don't lag.
10. Ask direct questions to get nestmates who seem reluctant to talk.
11. Stop personal attacks.
12. Stop chicken-fights.
13. At the close of the meeting, review what has been discussed.
14. Make certain each nester knows what behaviors are expected as a result of this meeting.
15. Write down specific behaviors for each nester to remember, or post reminders of the meeting results in a place where nest members will be reminded.
16. Have grain (and plenty of it).
17. Meet in a relaxing part of the nest.
18. Meet at a relaxed time.
19. Meet at a convenient time.
20. Create ownership in the meeting.

"Precision of communication is important, more important than ever, in our era of hair-trigger balances, when a false or misunderstood word may create as much disaster as a sudden thoughtless act."

James Thurber

8

> *"A hedge between keeps friendship green."*
>
> German Proverb

Sample Letter of Invitation to a Nest Meeting

Dear Clur-Eggs:

We like to have you with us. We want our nest to be a place where each of us feels comfortable and enjoys living. We want our nest to be a peaceful, loving place where each of us can feel good and grow.

We think that most of the time this is the kind of nest we have. In the past few weeks, we have been getting careless about the way we treat each other, our nest, our cars and our outside areas. When we are careless, this causes the chick and rooster to have to squawk and scold, and causes the eggs to fracture with fighting.

So that we can live peacefully together, love each other and have fun together, we'd like to work together on some reminders about nest rules which will help us be responsible to each other. Caring about our nestmates, the nest, the cars, and the neighbors in the chickenyard is an important part of growing and living in a nest.

We'd like to call a nest meeting for breakfast. We will fix breakfast together (see the list of responsibilities), and then we will have a nest discussion and do some exercises to help us get back on track as a nest working together for success.

We are proud of our eggs, and we are proud of our nest. We love it when other chickens notice how well-behaved, polite and courteous you have become. We are proud every time someone tells us how you contribute at church and at school. We are glad you have many friends and like a lot of different eggs. We are pleased that you work hard on egg hygiene and dress.

We want to continue to grow together and be a happy nest. Thank you for working with us to make this happen.

We love you!

The Chick and the Rooster

Breakfast Menu and List of Responsibilities

Eggs	Dad and Cam
Bacon	Dad and Ross
Toast	Dad, Cam, and Ross
Table setting	Stephanie and R-A
Breakfast mood music	Stephanie and R-A
Juice and coffee	Stephanie and R-A
Clean-up/table area	Stephanie and Dad
Clean-up/counter area	Cam and R-A
Clean-up/stove	Cam and R-A
Clean-up/load dishwasher	Dad and Ross

Nest-Meeting Format

Topic: _____

_____

Purpose: _____

_____

Date: _____

Location: _____

Food: _____

Materials: _____

_____

Agenda

Topic   *Topic Presenter*

1. _____   _____
2. _____   _____
3. _____   _____
4. _____   _____
5. _____   _____

Because I Care About This Nest, I Will Be Responsible

1. What does caring mean?

   _____

   _____

   _____

2. When I care about a person, how do I treat that person?

   _____

   _____

   _____

3. Because I live in a stepnest, with nestmates I care about, I have responsibilities to myself and to my nestmates.

   A. It is my responsibility to be pleasant.

      How can I be pleasant to nestmates?

      _____

      _____

      _____

   B. It is my responsibility to learn rules for chicken-fighting.

      Here are some good rules for chicken-fighting.

      _____

      _____

      _____

   C. It is my responsibility to respect others.

      How do I act toward nestmates to show that I respect them?

      _____

      _____

      _____

D. It is my responsibility to respect the area(s) where I live.

What things can I do that show that I respect the nestmates with whom I share the bathroom?

_____

_____

_____

What things can I do to show that I respect the nestmates with whom I share the bedroom?

_____

_____

_____

What things would you like those nestmates who share the bedroom and bathroom with you to do to show that they respect you?

_____

_____

_____

List some responsibilities that you would like to have for general nest maintenance in other areas of the nest, yard and garage that will help us be proud of our nest areas. What things would you like to keep looking nice for our nestmates and the rest of the yard?

_____

_____

_____

Make three basic rules for our nest to go by that will help us show each other that we care and are responsible for each other.

1. _____

_____

_____

8

2. _____
_____
_____

3. _____
_____
_____

These are sample titles for rule sheets that can be posted after completing the "Because I Live in this Nest" worksheet.

- Rules for Caring: Car/Van Riders
- Rules for Living Together in Our Bedroom
- Rules for Caring: Bathroom Users
- Rules for a Happy Nest
- Rules for Fighting
- Nest Responsibilities I Will Volunteer For

After our initial meeting, I laminated and framed the rules, placing them in the areas where they were to be remembered. Stephanie actually thanked me for doing this. She was also the first one to ask for the next family meeting. Eggs often seem to feel left out of family policy making. The youngest are the ones who most like to address injustices they feel others are heaping on them. They like the opportunity to air feelings and find positive action to cope with their difficulties.

The frequency with which you hold meetings will depend on how successful you find them and how much you have to discuss. Even the little eggs can sit through a family meeting and get used to this format. You may occasionally have to stop to recapture a runaway eighteen-month-old, but you may need the comic relief at the moment.

When this tool is begun early in the life of your nest, it becomes a tool that produces an atmosphere of fairness, negotiation, partnering and ownership. Any nest member should be able to ask for a nest meeting.

Nest meetings should be held for positive reasons: to improve a situation, to partner, to teach, to negotiate, to seek fairness, to praise. If every time a nest meeting is called, you know there is trouble, this tool will quickly become ineffective and unpleasant.

The eggs said after our first nest family meetings, "We like being able to talk about these things. It's fair here." Steph says, "When the boys do something to me, you make them stop and talk to me about it and change what they are doing. That makes it more fairer." Nests and individual members of nests have a right to expect fairness from their group. Nest meetings can be a great fairness tool.

How Do I Talk with the Eggs?

This is a question even biologically intact nests struggle with. Over time and the establishing of relationships, you won't be able to shut the eggs up. They bubble over with information. It doesn't begin like this. It takes a great deal of work. We have great communication in our nest now, but it was not always like this.

When I used to go pick up the eggs from day care for our overnight stays or for weekends, I always worried about what to talk about and how to keep the conversation going when we first got in the car. I assumed that this was a necessary part of relationship building.

I can remember painful Wednesday and Friday afternoons where we rode in a silent car with some people sleeping even after my attempts to start a conversation. I would even buy flavored soft drinks to try to loosen us up.

I always felt inadequate at these times. I had never had any trouble getting eggs to talk to me when I was teaching. What was wrong now? Steve kept telling me, "Parenting is different from teaching" and "Don't worry, they don't talk to me, either."

In frustration, I began buying story tapes to listen to on the way home and to and from school. Then I began sneaking in motivational tapes. We would listen to the tape for a while and then stop it to talk about what we were hearing. I found out so much about what they believed by doing this. We never lacked for conversation. Steve began to say, "How do you know so much more about these guys than I do? Why do they talk to you and not to me? I can't get two words out of them even when I question them."

The tapes provided a beginning and some thought material that stimulated interesting and informative conversation. Now we find it easy to talk about almost anything.

> *"Problems should be utilized. If you've never been unhappy, how would you know what happy is?"*
>
> Malcolm Forbes

What are some other tips for having conversation with your eggs?

8

Twenty Tips for More Successful Conversations with Your Stepegg

1. *Listen to your eggs without judging them.*

   The active listening technique of reflective listening is great here. Simply listen and occasionally repeat a piece of what the egg is saying. Example:

Egg:	"That test in Spanish today was really easy. I'm sure I aced it."
Chick:	"So it was a pretty easy test, huh?"
Egg:	"Yeah, except for how I spelled one word, I'm sure I got it all right."

2. *When your eggs are talking, keep them talking by asking open-ended questions.*

   "Tell me about..."
   "Describe..."
   "Explain..."
   "How do you feel about..."
   "What do you think about..."

3. *Take body language into consideration as you listen. Does it match the words?*

Egg:	"I'm really enjoying band." (Said with slumping posture and a very weak smile.)
Rooster:	"So band is going great?"
Egg:	"Well, there are nine percussionists and he's only going to choose three. Some of those kids have been taking private lessons for four or five years. I've hardly played at all."
Rooster:	"So some of those kids are pretty good?"
Egg:	"Uh-huh. I wonder if I should transfer to art. I'm pretty good at art."

Rooster: "You think you want to transfer out of band and into art."

Egg: "Yeah. Could you go with me tomorrow to sign for a schedule change?"

Nest discussion question:

What if this rooster had simply listened to the words?

(Use this discussion question to teach a simple version of active listening to each family member, perhaps in a family meeting. Point out how interesting it can be to really get to know more about another.)

4. Question with interest, not interrogation.

"That was really a tough situation. How did you handle it?"

not

"Did you immediately deny that accusation?"

5. Try to put yourself in their place as you listen.

What's happening in this egg's life at this moment that could be impacting behavior and communication?

6. Monitor your own filters as you listen.

Is it really the fact that he didn't pick up his dirty socks, or does that hair style just get to you?

7. Check your nonverbal behavior as you listen. Does it "look" as if you are interested and nonjudgmental?

Are you watching the evening news with one eye and making monosyllabic responses, or are you making eye contact with your egg and using reflective listening?

8. Avoid putting yourself in a superior position as you listen.

"Well, if I'd been there, I'd have..."

"The human animal needs a freedom seldom mentioned, freedom from intrusion. He needs a little privacy quite as much as he wants understanding or vitamins or exercise or praise."

Phyllis McGinley

8

8

9. *Give other chickens a chance to talk.*

10. *Share stories of similar situations in your own life.*

   (Just don't use them as one-uppers.)

11. *Listen between the lines.*

   What is the emotional mood of this egg?
   What time of day is it?
   Is there a history with this issue?

12. *Avoid talking down.*

   "Do you get it?"
   "Are you sure you understood what the teacher meant?"
   "Let me help you say this better."

13. *Avoid sermonizing.*

   Keep your responses short.

14. *Use "I" messages.*

   "I'm really upset about this."
                           not
   "You make me so angry."

15. *Listen for the real problem underneath the petty issues.*

   "So there must be something else bothering you."

16. *Be firm, but be willing to negotiate.*

   "We need to take action on this. What would you recommend?"

17. *Encourage personal problem-solving.*

   "What do you think you should do first?"

18. *Avoid finishing their sentences for them.*

    This tells them you feel that you know better what's in their head than they do.

19. *Ask for specifics.*

    "So all 1600 kids at school tomorrow are wearing purple shoes." *(In response to the "everyone's doing this" argument.)*

20. *Find things you can laugh about together.*

(By the way, these twenty hints work with your spouse too.)

Establish Communication and Feedback with a Stepchick or Rooster Mentor

Isn't it strange how being able to talk to another stepchick or rooster who has been through what you're going through is a tremendous relief? It helps to know that you are not alone, that other nests have experienced the pains, joys and frustrations that you are experiencing.

> *"Let our scars fall in love."*
>
> Galloway Kinnel

Finding a mentor can save your life and your mind (perhaps also your nest) and will definitely improve your relationship with the eggs. Some of the mentors you will talk with to share, expose and expunge anger. Some will be able to suggest solutions that worked for them, simple concepts that relieve complicated situations and tools for success that could work in your nest.

No matter what your situation, there are common threads that run through the stepnest experience. What kind of person(s) would you choose for a mentor?

Profile of a Mentor

1. A person of balance
   (Someone who is not still terribly angry)

2. A person who is a healthy match between your needs and their experiences

   For example:
   Raising teenage or preadolescent boys is different than raising teenage or preadolescent girls.

   So, to find your match, you need to be clear about your needs and find the person who has the right experience base to match your needs.

3. A person willing to listen

4. A person willing to share

5. A person of candor

6. A person who is caring

8

Mentor Worksheet

1. Why am I seeking a mentor?

   _____
   _____
   _____

2. What are the specific needs that I wish to discuss with my mentor?

   _____
   _____
   _____

3. What do I hope for as a result of spending time with this mentor?

   _____
   _____
   _____

4. How long do I want to work with this mentor?

   _____
   _____
   _____

5. How often do I need to meet with my mentor?

   _____
   _____
   _____

6. What arrangements do I need to set up front with my mentor?

   _____
   _____
   _____

> *"Few people are capable of expressing with equanimity opinions which differ from the prejudices of their social environment. Most people are even incapable of forming such opinions."*
>
> Albert Einstein

8

This guideline sheet will be helpful to you before you seek your mentor. It is fair to be able to share this information with the person you ask to mentor you. A mentor will want to know that you will not be calling him/her at all hours of the day and night unless there is some kind of emergency. Arranging some specific times in advance gives this mentoring relationship some professional qualities and significance that it may not have unless these arrangements are made and understood up front.

Some people are so busy that they will hesitate to take on yet another responsibility no matter how important they think this responsibility actually is.

The stepchicks and roosters who have mentored me are people who have been kind enough to take just a few minutes on the phone whenever we happened to be talking about something else. They have asked a simple question such as, "How are the eggs?" and my needs, thoughts and emotions have come pouring out. I call them "on-the-spot" healers and mentors. You will have and need these too. I often have wondered, though, what if I had arranged on a regular basis to meet with these wise and experienced people to get feedback and suggestions early on in my stepchick experience? Would we have been able to solve problems earlier or take proactive rather than reactive approaches? I think the answer to that is definitely, "Yes!"

Summary: Nest-Communication Rules Continue to Change

We recently got physical custody of our two boys. Some of the rules which worked before still work. Others had to be developed and some had to be redefined.

Any growing organism like a nest changes constantly. Your rules and the clarity of your rules will change over time. Helping the eggs with definitions early on, modeling clearly defined roles and spaces helps them for later, when the definitions and redefining become their responsibility. Another stepchick friend of mine with hatched stepeggs says, "I don't have to worry any more about the fact that the biochick wants them to come for some time in the summer and they don't want to. Their relationship with her and how they choose to define it is up to them now."

When your communication is established in your nest unit, you can then use some of your guidelines to have functional communication with the extended yard.

Bernard Baruch has said, "The ability to express an idea is well nigh as important as the idea itself." If you substitute the word "feeling" for the word "idea" in this quotation, you get a key to successful stepnest functioning. You need vehicles for feeling expression, tools for appropriate expression of the feeling and freedom to do the expressing.

Communication holds stepnests together. Rules for communication both spoken and written give the stepnest consistency, create respect and allow space to grow. Once the chickenyard is ordered, it is a cleaner, healthier, freer space to be.

"Let every man be respected as an individual and no man idolized."

Albert Einstein

8

8

*C*HAPTER 9

Manage Conflict with Fair Chicken-Fighting

"Does anyone really win?"

"Responsibility is to keep the ability to respond."

Gustav Mahler

Am I in This "Stuff" Alone?

Remember when you were a kid and you'd had a fight with one or both of your parents? You could have been anywhere between the ages of three and sixteen. You'd run and throw yourself on the floor of your closet, close the door just enough that you were confident of being able to open it if you really needed to get out and sit there thinking to yourself, "It would serve them right if I died. Then they'd be sorry for how they treat me. Nobody here loves me anyway." Now is that truly childish behavior or what?

Ever found yourself in a similar situation as a stepchick or rooster? I have. It may not be the closet these days. It can be long walks, late at night when you think, "I probably shouldn't be out here alone, but who cares? No one will be upset if something does happen to me." It's storming away from the house carrying a book under your shirt and climbing up to the shelter of the fort in the top of the big toy at the park not far from your house. Sitting there batting away the little eggs who think they have a right to be there and trying to read, you think, "How did I get myself into this situation and do I want to get out?"

> *"Very few people are such complete self-starters that they can make it without any help."*
>
> Robert Beck

> *"It is better to have one person working with you than three people working for you."*
>
> Dwight D.
> Eisenhower

9

Sometimes when you're in the mood to escape, it has more to do with a disagreement with the chick or rooster than with the eggs. But often, it stems from a conflict you had with one of the eggs in which the chick or rooster chose to intervene and override. You feel totally left out, totally useless, totally devalued and very alone.

The Yard in Chaos

Conflict occurs on many levels even in biologically intact nests. In stepnests, with all filters operational, feelings on shirtsleeves and chips on wings, conflict seems to be frequent, explosive, hurtful and divisive. The chickenyard erupts, eggs get mushed, roosters rush and scream, hens get their feathers ruffled and run to the nest for protection. You have conflict "because of" everything and everyone. You can blame your conflict on your situation and wallow in it or you can take responsibility for using your conflict to learn and grow together, not apart.

You have conflict with biochicks and roosters over schedules, who pays little league fees and did you really agree to split that doctor's fee? Conflict with the extended yard comes when they are determined to harp on the fact that everyone in the situation must somehow be damaged, insist that "she's probably allowing them to live with you just because they're really a problem at her house — you really should investigate this," and continually point out, "well, she is the mother."

You have conflict with the eggs who say (at least in the beginning stages), "You're not my Mom/Dad," and you want to yell back, "And, thank God for that! If you were acting this way and had my genes I'd be seriously examining the emotional stability of my family tree!"

Eggs have conflict with each other and chicks and roosters have conflict. You sometimes seem to be just one big garbled mass of hormonal difficulties, tangled family-tree limbs, egg rivalry, marital strife, in-law interference and general interpersonal difficulty. How do you survive without going and checking the entire nest (ex and extended included) into the nearest mental-health facility?

Many nests look for outside fixes. They turn to counselors, social agencies, teachers and churches to take care of the problems they are having inside the nest. While all of these resources can be helpful, the problems will not truly be solved until you learn internal conflict management. You need to fix the chickenyard from the inside out. Having others rearrange the yard structure and interview the inhabitants will not solve the problem until the inhabitants want the problem solved enough to start digging themselves.

Take the First Chicken-Step

First you need to understand that conflict is a normal, healthy part of everyday life. Understand the:

Four Truths Our Stepnest Accepts About Chicken-fights

1. Chicken-fights are normal and can produce growth, learning and creative solutions.

2. Respect each egg, chick or rooster's right to express disagreement and respond rather than react when nestmates disagree.

3. Solve problems with the appropriate nestmate in an attitude of respect for that nester.

4. Depersonalize your chicken-fights by following established procedures for chicken-fighting.

> *"Without feelings of respect, what is there to distinguish men from beasts?"*
> Confucius

As you examine each of these Truths, keep an open mind to changing your mind about conflict and producing greater peace and learning opportunities for your nest.

1. Chicken fights are normal and can produce growth, learning and creative solutions.

Every time you have conflict with another nester, you learn something about what he cares about. You don't go to the wall for things you do not care about. If you fight with me about

> *"If you have some respect for people as they are, you can be more effective in helping them to become better than they are."*
>
> John Gardner

an issue, you have shown me a new part of yourself. This is something you care about. Even if the issue itself is not a big deal, you have cared enough about yourself that you chose to defend yourself to me by defending your issue. Questions I can ask myself while you are defending yourself are:

1. Is it this issue that she really cares about and is defending?

2. Is it herself that she really cares about and is defending?

Asking these questions while listening helps you depersonalize and step emotionally away from this conflict.

When Ross and Steve and I were in conflict over Ross's personal-responsibility issues, we helped work on the conflict issues to help develop his art skills. The letter we wrote him shows how.

Our Responsibility Letter to Ross

Dear Ross:

Since art is a strong talent that you have, let's use that talent to help you manage an area which you are finding difficult. Remember the times that you have...

- Not finished putting away materials you used in making your lunch

- Forgotten to close the car door

- Left things in the car

- Left things in your room that you needed for school and had to run at the last minute?

You can probably remember a number of times that you have not put all the steps of a process together so that you could be successful.

Let's take your art talent and use it to help you develop a series of checklists for processes that you routinely perform. Here are some examples of how this could work:

- Make a checklist for making a lunch, from getting things out to putting things away and all the steps in between.
- Make a checklist for getting ready for school from waking up to getting in the car and arriving at school.
- Make a checklist for homework that needs to be done.
- Make a checklist for home chores and the steps that need to be done.

Maybe when you develop these checklists in an organized way and use your artistic talents to decorate them, it will help you and others to remember all the steps you need to be successful.

Begin with the checklist that is the thing you most often get in trouble about. Have a goal of developing three checklists this weekend. Here's what "develop" means:

Make a list (in time order) of all the functions this task requires.

- Have Dad or R-A check the list.

- Revise the list if needed.

- Put the list on one of your sheets of sketchbook paper.

- Artistically, colorfully decorate the checklist.

We will take this list to KINKO's and have it laminated so that it can be placed where you need it (kitchen, bathroom, bedroom, notebook for school).

Each time we notice that you need a management suggestion or help with self-management, we will ask you to make another checklist. This will give you a way to jog your thought processes about how to complete tasks from top to bottom with success.

Thank you for your cooperation in using your talents to manage your areas which need improvement.

Love,

Dad & R-A.

> *"What concerns everyone can only be resolved by everyone."*
> Friedrich Durrenmatt

9

"Problems are only opportunities in work clothes."

Henry J. Kaiser

9

Conflict is a time when writing is sometimes better than direct oral confrontation. Having these issues written down, dated and documented also lets you check on your follow-through and the follow-through of the eggs. Systems set in place in the nest do very little good unless there is follow-through. Conflict can actually increase when you discuss solutions that never become real.

2. Respect each egg, chick or rooster's right to express disagreement and respond rather than react when nestmates disagree.

In your family, this truth about responding rather than reacting has something to do with the tone of voice and body language you use when disagreeing. Work hard and continually on speaking to nestmates with respectful tones. Harsh and condemning squawking is a reaction. Respectful clucking is a response.

Work on having calm, unruffled feathers. Relaxed body language which says, "I am listening with respect," de-escalates conflict and is a response rather than a reaction. Even very young eggs can be taught to use gentle voice tones. They can also be taught through on-the-spot coaching to "let your body go soft" when they feel themselves getting angry or tense. They can also be coached immediately when a nestmate observes the egg getting angry or tense.

Talk to the nest about controlling, name-calling, labeling and language that is hurtful and inflammatory during times of tension. When an egg plays computer games on the chick's work computer and wipes out the printer function while the chick is trying to meet an editing deadline, it is tempting to say, "I can't believe you are that stupid and inconsiderate!" It is better to say, "I am in a very difficult situation because of what has happened here today. I need to know how you plan to help me fix this."

3. Solve problems with the appropriate nestmate in an attitude of respect for that nester.

Stepnest relationships get very complicated. When you tattle to the biochick or rooster about what an egg has done instead of dealing with the egg yourself, you run the risk of the biochick/ rooster feeling defensive about the egg. Now you have a battle between the chick and the rooster because of the egg.

When a stepegg tattles on a bioegg (or vice versa) to a chick or rooster, there is always the suspicion that blood will win out or that biologically related nestmates always defend each other and favor each other. Eggs need to deal appropriately and directly with other eggs, and chicks and roosters need to deal appropriately and directly with eggs.

The fewer go-betweens involved in the conflict, the better. Using the, "I feel ... ," "Here's why ... ," "Here's what I think is fair ... " method will help make these messages fair, appropriate and direct.

4. **Depersonalize your chicken-fights by following established procedures for fighting.**

When the nest is in an uproar, some kind of prearranged time-out is helpful. You don't need to be flinging yard dirt at each other. You have been working to heal bruises. You don't need to inflict more by thoughtlessly flinging words and actions that will pile up and make the nest even more uncomfortable.

Rules that you work out when the nest is peaceful can provide the time-out when stress occurs. Go to the rules during the tense moments. Time yourselves out by stopping the altercation and reading the rules.

"Our problems are man-made, therefore they may be solved by man. And man can be as big as he wants. No problem of human destiny is beyond human beings."

John F. Kennedy

9

General Rules for Conflict Resolution

A. Listen carefully.

B. If you hear hints that something else might be wrong other than the issue you're discussing, ask about what else might be wrong.

1. "I wonder if you're angry because I got my room painted and you didn't?"
2. "It seems there must be something else bothering you."

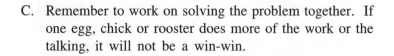

9

C. Remember to work on solving the problem together. If one egg, chick or rooster does more of the work or the talking, it will not be a win-win.

D. Talk in a neutral place where no chick, egg or rooster feels threatened. Meeting in one nestmate's corner of the nest puts him in a more powerful position.

E. Begin with stating the purpose of your discussion. "Mark, we need to talk about our disagreement over who cuts the lawn this time."

Chicks and roosters who are disagreeing with each other or mediating a disagreement should follow the "Tips for Mediating Chicken-Fights." The "Chicken-Fights Management Worksheet" can be used by any nest member of any age who can read and write. Chicks, roosters and older eggs can ask eggs who can't read or write yet the questions on the "Conflict Management Worksheet." The earlier this work is begun, the better. It helps eggs (and chicks and roosters) learn sooner to work things out rather than fight them out. You might try using these guidelines in your nest.

Tips for Mediating Chicken-Fights

1. Be able to get conflict communication going without feeling threatened as the chick or rooster.

2. Point out ways the fighters agree in the beginning of the mediation process.

3. Ask each "fighter" to put himself in the other nestmate's place. (Where appropriate, this could be done on paper.)

   A. How might you feel?
   B. How might you react?

   (This step is especially important if one of the "fighters" is a chick or rooster. How can you manage your own conflicts?)

4. Look for ways to strengthen relationships through chicken-fight situations.

   A. The chick and rooster should apologize.
   B. The chick and rooster can be understanding.
   C. The chick and/or rooster can take the first step toward resolution.

5. Use paraphrasing to understand all sides.

   "Is this what you mean?"

   "What I feel you just said was..."

   "I'd like to understand. Is this what you are saying?"

6. Make it clear that you want a solution that each nestmate involved can accept.

7. Understand that this conflict is about things or ideas, not chicks, eggs or roosters.

8. State your side without giving a lecture about why you are right.

9. Use reflective statements to get at feelings.

   A. Example of a reflective statement.

      Egg: I'm trying to clean the room. I have my part clean, but Ross is such a pig that his side is still a mess. He keeps messing around and leaving the room all the time before he's finished.

      Rooster: You're pretty angry with Ross.

> *"The measure of success is not whether you have a tough problem to deal with, but whether it's the same problem you had last year."*
>
> John Foster Dulles

9

187

> *"All problems become smaller if, instead of indulging them, you confront them. Touch a thistle timidly and it pricks you; grasp it boldly, and its spine crumbles.*
>
> William S. Halsey

B. Advantages of a reflective statement:

  1. Nestmate feels understood.
  2. Nestmate is invited to explore his feelings.
  3. Nestmate can let off steam.
  4. Rapport is created.

10. Seek a neutral mediator if necessary.

"Solve it. If you need help (a negotiator), call me."

11. Time-outs may be necessary.

12. When you have been the mediator, seek honest, caring, nonjudgmental feedback from your spouse about:

  A. the chicken-fight itself
  B. the source of the chicken-fight
  C. your management of the chicken-fight

Important chicken-fighting rule to remember:
  Attack problems, not nestmates.

When you are involved in chicken-fights or are mediating them, the Chicken-Fighting Management Worksheet is one that each fighter should fill out before proceeding with the mediation or negotiation. It provides a time-out and information needed for successful mediation.

Chicken-Fighting Management Worksheet

1. What are some of the things we agree about

   _____

   _____

   _____

2. If I were in _____'s place, how would I feel?

   _____

   _____

   _____

3. What do I wish would happen in this situation?

   _____

   _____

   _____

4. Right now I feel ...

   _____

   _____

   _____

5. I would feel better if ...

   _____

   _____

   _____

6. One thing I really like about _____ is ...

   _____

   _____

   _____

7. I will ...

   _____

   _____

   _____

> *"After all, a smooth sea never made a successful sailor."*
>
> Herman Melville

9

and he will ...

_____

_____

_____

After getting this basic information, some nest members may choose to draft a "Rules for Fair Chicken-Fighting" agreement. I have included ours as an example.

Rules for Fair Chicken-Fighting

1. Try to work it out between yourselves.
2. Explain what you thought they said.
3. Listen.
4. Go to another area of the nest to cool off.
5. When playing games, talk about rules first.
6. Remember some egg has to give in.
7. Keep squawking down.
8. Ask the other egg, chick, rooster to explain why he/she is angry.
9. Work together.
10. Compromise to solve the problem.
11. Shake wings or fluff feathers.
12. Let both eggs tell their side of the story. Then try to solve it.

Getting the Chick or Rooster Who Is Your Adversary to See Your Point of View

It helps to have specific rules for dealing with biochicks and roosters. They often take the position of adversary. They may not choose to take this position — it may be one we assign to them. On the other hand, they may enjoy it a great deal. So what are the tips for dealing with an adversary? By the way, we can also use these when dealing with the extended yard and might even choose to adapt a few when the adversary is a member of the immediate stepnest.

9

"The greater the difficulty, the greater the glory."

Cicero

Getting the Adversarial Chick or Rooster to See Your Point of View

A. Only make statements you can support.
B. Support your statements with evidence the adversary will recognize and respect.
C. Clearly outline points of disagreement.
D. Ask for something you have a chance of getting.
E. Show that you understand his side too.
F. Show how each of you can win.
G. Point out common ground before discussing disagreement.
H. Show how what you want is also in the best interest of your adversary.
I. Pray that some of this will work!

> *"Problems are not stop signs, they are guidelines."*
>
> Robert Schuller

9

Summary: Be Committed to Your Relationships Rather Than to Winning Chicken-Fights, Realizing That You Cannot Really Change Anyone but Yourself.

This whole chapter is designed to point out that nest relationships are more important than the tally on the yard wall of wins and losses. For example, my mother and I are so much alike that it has caused us controversy all my life. We are both very strong-willed, certain that we are right and determined to persuade others to agree with us. I remember several nights as a child when Mom and I had really had a serious disagreement. Mom would always come in just after I got in bed. She would hug me, tell me she loved me and say she was sorry we had disagreed in the way that we had. I learned that it was OK to disagree and still love someone.

We continued to disagree about many things for a long time. In the last few years, we have decided to accept each other for who we are and value our relationship with each other more than our opinions. This has not been something we have ever discussed — it has just happened. It has made us better friends than we have ever been.

> *"To overcome difficulties is to experience the full delight of existence."*
>
> Arthur Schopenhauer

I remember a conscious moment when I said to myself, "Mom is who she is. I will love her for that. She is truly authentic and does not act unless she feels she is doing what is right. I will accept her actions as authentic representations of herself and not expect her to change to please me." I don't know if her flash was similar, but it has obviously occurred. We discuss these days instead of argue. We even choose not to discuss some things which are inflammatory because we hold our relationship too dear to endanger it over an idea.

I wish I had received my flash earlier, but having gotten it, I use it with other members of my nest both immediate and extended. It beats hiding in forts and closets.

9

*C*HAPTER 10

Discipline to Raise Happy, Positive and Productive Eggs

"It never ends!"

Birthing is a biological process.
Parenting is a conscious choice.

"The difficulty in life is the choice."

George Moore

There's More to It Than Laying the Eggs

Many types of organisms can become biological parents. Chicks and roosters of all ages can become biological parents. What's important to the future of the eggs and the yard is, do those biological parents choose to really be parents?

"Why do so few people choose to parent? Lots of people choose to birth."

"Why don't people realize that God gave children parents for a reason?"

"Why is it so hard to say 'no?'"

"How can people expect the school, church and community to do it all?"

Heard these comments at parties recently, or among neighbors conversing, or in the coffee shop, or in the myriad classes on

> *"Do not consider painful what is good for you."*
>
> Euripides

parenting that have sprung up everywhere? The comments seem to come mostly from baby boomers raised, as I was, with a mom who I firmly believed was hiding a military commander's experience somewhere in her background and a dad who set standards, taught us those standards and enforced those standards.

I remember comments from my childhood such as:

"Ruth-Ann, the fact that you are a teenager does not mean that the rest of us are going to suffer."

My mom

"If you get in trouble at school, you will get in twice as much trouble when you get home."

My dad

"Never forget that you are a Lawrence."

My grandfather Lawrence

"You can get glad in the same pants you got mad in."

My grandmother Bernson

I was raised with fairness. I knew the rules, I knew what happened if I obeyed the rules, and I knew what happened if I broke the rules. I knew there were parents and grandparents in my life who had certain expectations regarding my behavior. I will never forget the times before we visited my Lawrence grandparents when my mother drilled us for weeks on proper behavior.

My grandparents were "of the old school" that children were expected to behave by high standards at all times. There were certain table manners to be observed, adults were to be respected at all times, you didn't fight with your siblings, you were quiet while being transported by car to your next destination and never, never did you cause any trouble in church!

At home, we didn't even have a television until I was twelve. We were abused by having to read books. (A habit, by the way, which has brought me professional success and personal happiness.) When we finally got a TV, my parents allowed us to watch one and a half hours a week. We chose the shows at the beginning of the week and stuck to those decisions.

When cigarette or beer commercials came on, we were required to turn down the sound and not look at the screen until those commercials were over. Usually my brother Mark solved this issue for all of us by standing in front of the TV and periodically peeking over his shoulder to see if the commercial was over yet.

We were raised very strictly and with a lot of love. We never went to bed without a hug and kiss from both parents and any grandparents who were present. (On the other hand, one of the worst punishments my siblings and I ever got was to have to hug and kiss after a fight. Yuck!) Now, of course, we siblings hug without being told and love each other a great deal. We are, in fact, best friends. There are four of us, and we often talk about our strict discipline. We also talk about the fact that we seem to have turned out alright. The keys to success with discipline lie in very simple guidelines whether the family is biologically intact or step.

The "Ten Disciplinary Success Guidelines" are clear and fair. They take advance thought and work on the part of the chick and the rooster. "The Disciplinary Standards Necessary for Nest Success" worksheet later in this chapter will help you develop your own definitions of each of these standards.

Ten Disciplinary Success Guidelines

1. Be willing to discipline.
2. Be consistent and fair.
3. Make neither chick nor rooster the heavy.
4. Set standards.
5. Communicate the standards orally to the eggs.
6. Put the standards in writing and go over them with the eggs.
7. Determine consequences for violating the standards.
8. Establish rewards when standards are met or exceeded.
9. Train eggs using the standards.
10. Evaluate egg behavior based on the standards.

These guidelines would work in bio- or stepnests. What are some of the extra considerations that the stepnest must look at?

10

> *"If men live decently, it is because discipline saves their very lives for them."*
>
> Sophocles

> *"Set thine house in order."*
>
> Isaiah 38:1

Additional Guidelines for Stepparenting Discipline

1. Establish the "in-this-nest" mentality.

A good reason for rules in writing in each area where those rules are to be noted is that rules vary for eggs from nest to nest. We have always answered the, "...but Mom doesn't make us do this..." plaint with, "In this house we...." That separates the nests just as laundry is separated. Eggs need to know that throughout their lives there will be different standards in different places. No two jobs will have the same standards. We often use the analogy that different teachers from year to year and class to class have different standards.

Different standards are not wrong, just different. The more concretely the rules are defined and explained, the easier it will be to appreciate and know the differences.

2. Insist that good manners and discipline be practiced everywhere.

"When you are in this house, these are the rules. We will expect you to use these standards any time you are in this house or in our company outside of this house."

3. Have contracts, especially with eggs who visit only periodically.

If standards are not in writing, it makes it easy for visiting eggs to say, "You didn't tell me that." When standards are written and contracts are drawn up together, there is documentation. Contracts may even need to be posted in a common area. Contracts may also be discussed over the phone and put in writing prior to the nest visitation of the egg(s).

Here's an example of two of ours:

Ruth-Ann,

I promise to:

1. Not fool around at the Java Stop
2. Not act up during any duration of this trip to Washington D.C.
3. Act like I was raised by the Queen of England
4. Listen to you at all times
5. Abide by my time schedule

Ross Clurman

(Can you tell the eggs wrote these themselves?)

> **"Order is heaven's first law."**
>
> Alexander Pope

10

Contract

NAME:	Cameron Lee Clurman
AGE:	14 years old
JOB:	Java Stop
BIRTH:	11/2/80
DATE:	7/9/95

I, Cameron Clurman, will obey all commands and instructions given to me by my elders at work, school and at home. I will do my chores to the best of my ability and will do them right. I will not goof off at serious moments and won't play around with inventions that can hurt and even kill someone. I will be a responsible person and won't go back on my word.

(You can probably also tell that sometimes these contracts are written AFTER an offense has been committed, as part of the disciplinary process.)

4. **Have the same rules and expectations for all eggs in the house.**

    A. Those who live in this nest all the time
    B. Those who visit this nest periodically

When eggs are visiting, it is easy for the chick and rooster to view them as guests. The eggs who live in the nest all the time, begin to feel that they are being treated unfairly when their normal chores and expectations are continuing while the "guest egg" is simply "recreating." Far from feeling "put upon," the visiting egg will feel more an actual part of this nest when there are expectations of load sharing. Chicks and roosters in stepnests cannot afford to simply be the recreational nest. This philosophy takes a serious toll on all concerned. Unresolved resentment builds and becomes a serious crack in the nest!

5. Work out disciplinary guidelines as chick and rooster; then

6. Partner eggs in setting standards.

It is important for the chick and rooster to present a united front to ALL eggs. Fractures in all nestmates and the nest itself happen when the chick or rooster (behind the other's back) say to eggs, "Oh well, she is just being a little squawky today. If you just lay low, she will come out of it. Don't worry about this." Worse yet is the chick or rooster who says, "We'll just do it our way; she will catch on sooner or later." And most awful for the eggs are those moments when the chick and rooster openly and loudly squawk to each other about their differences of disciplinary opinion in front of the eggs. This causes the eggs to be insecure and crack. It causes almost irreparable damage to the relationship of the chick and rooster in the nest.

When the Chick and Rooster Don't Agree

Here's a comment I heard in my stepparenting workshops:

"How can I encourage her when we don't agree? She doesn't believe the behavior needs correction, and I do, or vice versa."

This comment is a perfect example of why the chick and rooster need to have a standard-setting session. At this time, negotiation can occur. Both the chick and the rooster need to keep the welfare of the eggs in mind. What is best in the long run for the nest? It is easy to say, "Oh well. They're not here all the time. Let's just let it go." Or, "We only have about five years left with them. Let's just tough it out till then."

Stepnests cannot allow resentment to grow. These issues must be dealt with up front. If you are already in an established nest, it is still not too late to:

1. As chick and rooster, negotiate and set standards.
2. Have a family meeting that explains the new standards.
3. Ask for egg input.
4. Post the new standards.
5. Train using the new standard.
6. Evaluate egg behavior consistently, based on these standards.

The way you were disciplined often determines how you discipline. My dad was disciplined quite harshly as a child. He was firm, consistent, and fair but also determined that we would not have to spend all our waking moments working. He wanted us to learn to play and feel free to have leisure time.

The chick and rooster need to examine why they feel it is necessary to have a certain type of discipline. There may be reasons you are not even aware of. Sometimes getting to the bottom of these reasons will help resolve conflict in disciplinary styles as you realize why you are acting the way you are or are committed to a certain style. The Nest History worksheet in Chapter One will help with some of these answers.

The chick and rooster also need to examine why they are unwilling to let the other parent belong in this nest. When you don't have the right to discipline, you don't belong. You are not being given equality in a nest that you help support and helped to create. This disenfranchisement will lead to resentment on the part of the stepchick or rooster and chaos for the entire nest. If you're going to sit on these eggs and help hatch them, you have a right to some input about what kind of being emerges from the shells!

> *"As states subsist in part by keeping their weaknesses from being known, so is it the quiet of families to have their chancery and their parliament within doors, and to compose and determine all emergent difference there."*
>
> John Donne

10

"There is little less trouble in governing a private family than a whole kingdom."

Montaigne

10

Stepchicks and roosters need to examine themselves and make certain that their discipline comes from caring rather than from resentment. Eggs tolerate a lot of mistakes from biochicks and roosters and stepchicks and roosters when they know they are loved and cared for.

When chicks and roosters have decided on boundaries, they need to agree to support each other. Nothing undermines a stepchick or rooster's authority more or causes more hurtful feelings of not belonging than being unsupported or overridden in a disciplinary action.

Remember the comment that the counselor made to me early on in our marriage: "You are a parent figure whether you like it or not. You can't just be the friend." My willingness to discipline early and take the heat has made for very comfortable, friendly relationships with the eggs now. They will be the first to tell you that I am fair. That is the important part. The stepeggs must know that you like them, care about them and are administering discipline fairly rather than vengefully or to assuage resentment.

Rules in writing up front, consequences known up front and rewards administered evenhandedly help the eggs accept discipline.

Egg Disciplinary Steps Review

1. Always explain why an action is being taken.
2. Examine what has happened.
3. Establish that the egg knew this was unacceptable.
4. Remind the egg of the consequences.

When this review takes place, it is a reteaching of the standard, a reminder of the consequences and a reinforcement of the standard.

Maybe a brainstorming sheet would be helpful here as chicks and roosters begin, continue or revise this standard-setting process. Use this as a guide and add or delete as fits your family situation.

Disciplinary Standards Necessary for Nest Success

1. What standards are necessary regarding household chores?

    _____

    _____

    _____

    _____

    _____

2. What standards are necessary in areas outside of the nest?

    _____

    _____

    _____

    _____

    _____

3. What standards are necessary for table behavior?

    _____

    _____

    _____

    _____

    _____

4. What standards are necessary for behavior while riding in vehicles?

    _____

    _____

    _____

    _____

    _____

10

5. What standards are necessary regarding school?

_____

_____

_____

_____

_____

6. What standards are necessary regarding finance?

_____

_____

_____

_____

_____

7. What standards are necessary regarding health?

_____

_____

_____

_____

_____

8. What standards are necessary regarding personal privacy?

_____

_____

_____

_____

_____

9. What standards are necessary regarding respect of nestmates?

_____

_____

_____

_____

_____

10

10. What standards are necessary regarding use of time?

_____

_____

_____

_____

_____

This will get you started. You will have many others that you think of yourself. I have included some of our nest standards for your thought.

Rules for Scheduling Parties

1. Check to see that it is not a weekend that R-A is coming in on Friday and leaving again on Sunday.
2. Check with both Dad and R-A about the date.
3. Negotiate all details with one or both parents.
4. Write details down so we have good communication about it and can remember what we negotiated.
5. These are some of the details to be negotiated:
   A. How many people?
   B. What hours — start time and end time.
   C. What food?
   D. What activities?
6. The person who is having the party is responsible for cleaning up the house before and after the party. Here's what cleanup means:
   A. Vacuuming.
   B. Dusting.
   C. Straightening up.
   D. Lawn cleanup, mowing, etc.
   E. Garage cleanup if entering through this area.
   F. Kitchen readiness and clean-up.
7. The person having the party is responsible for food and drink preparation and cleanup. This person may contract and pay or arrange trades to have another person do this part for her.
8. Curfew will be set for overnights, and the person having the party is responsible to see that it is enforced.

10

9. When having an overnight, all guests are expected to abide by house rules, including the phone rules. Calls may not be placed or received after 10:00 p.m.
10. When overnights involve Sunday morning, inform guests that we will be attending church.

Eggs know when the nest is in an uproar. They don't need the chaos either. They will be relieved when some chick or rooster finally has the nerve to step up to bat and take control. They do want to be partnered in this process, however, and the more ownership of this new nest system they feel, the more they will respect and live by the system.

What If They Choose to Fly to the Other Nest?

Here's another comment that is common in workshops:

"I was very lax as a single mom with my children because I was fearful they would leave me and go be with their dad. Sharon is a product of my laxness."

The fear that the child will go live with the other parent is one that kids pick up on and manipulate. Let me remind you of a couple who were friends of mine. They really had it together on this issue. They had thought out in advance that this egg comment, "Fine! I'll just go live with my dad," might come up. They told the eggs, "You may react any way you choose to this action, but we are one. If you try to make us choose, we will choose each other."

This sounds tough, but you can either choose to parent or let your eggs jail you and hold you hostage. When they become your jailer, you begin to resent them and the entire nest structure will crack. Eggs do not want or need to be the boss. Chicks and roosters must have the courage to be willing to lose eggs in order to keep them. They'll be back, and if they don't come back, you have a peaceful structure for those who have decided to stay and live with fairness and respect.

> *"Bringing up a family should be an adventure, not an anxious discipline in which everybody is constantly graded for performance."*
>
> Milton R. Sapirstein

10

The Chick and Rooster Have the Right and Responsibility to Discipline the Eggs

This workshop comment shows you why it's necessary to reassert your disciplinary rights:

> *"We are now dealing with some respect issues with my son. I'm not sure where my husband fits in with fathering my son. My husband feels tied down because he's not sure where his place is in disciplining a teen. It's frustrating for both of us. We need some counsel and advice because it's affecting our relationship."*

It is an absolute chick and rooster responsibility to discipline and an absolute right of an egg to be disciplined. Chicks and roosters owe it to their eggs to help them be eggs others can enjoy being around.

Discipline Eggs with Fairness and Respect

At first, and with younger eggs, the chick and rooster need to set the rules.

As the nest structure develops or when dealing with older eggs, I believe partnering in the rules gives ownership of them. When you own a rule, you remember the rule and obey the rule. I learned this from years of setting rules with the students in my classroom on the first day.

I gave the students lists that had my rules on them. We could negotiate some of these rules, know which ones were nonnegotiable, and add others which would add to the climate of respect. When I followed this method, I had rule enforcers and reminders all over the room. When the goal was an attitude of fairness and productivity, kids were eager to cooperate. Those not eager to cooperate soon learned the consequences.

I had classes full of juvenile delinquents and academic failures in night and summer school who developed rules with me in these same ways. I will never forget the night that one of my students

> *"Before success in any man's life he is sure to meet with much temporary defeat and, perhaps, some failure. When defeat overtakes a man, the easiest and most logical thing to do is quit. That is exactly what the majority of men do."*
>
> Napoleon Hill

came to night school late. He was obviously on drugs, and, when I told him he needed to obey the rule that said he had to go get a late pass, he threatened to hit me. Four wrestlers on the front row stood up, formed a wall around me and said, "You will not touch this woman, or you will answer to us." At the end of class that evening, these same guys said, "We know him. He might be waiting for you in the parking lot. Let us walk you to your car."

When eggs help with rule setting, they take ownership and enforcement responsibility for themselves and others. It's to the benefit of the entire nest when eggs help with setting the rules. Most of the time they are happy to do this. They have been nursing little grudges because they feel that fairness is not always present. Writing rules together to create a fair, respectful environment is something they don't mind doing.

For those eggs who will not cooperate in the rule setting, simply remind them that they will be expected to go by these rules whether they help create them or not. If they choose not to have input, then you are assuming that they agree with and will abide by these rules anyway.

Writing rules can be as general as asking people to write down the rules they think are needed in this nest. They can be as specific as definite rules for each specific area of the nest and car(s). They can deal with certain behaviors they would like to see from specific nest members. Starting with a suggested rule sheet is a good way to get the nest thinking.

Rules Our Nest Needs

_____

_____

_____

_____

_____

_____

_____

_____

_____

_____

_____

Younger eggs may actually be able to have some rule input. In other cases they will go by the rules until such time as they are able to articulate their feelings and abbreviate, alter or add their own rules.

Give the Eggs the "Big Picture" Results

I have always explained the reasons for rules. For example: We have "no eating in the living room" because there are fabric sofas and nice carpeting. If those things have to be replaced there is no money for school clothes in the fall, Christmas presents or baseball fees and equipment in the summer. Then, when we want to have a really special time watching a movie together at home, we drape the coffee table with a huge beach towel and enjoy the special moment of eating in a forbidden place.

I have included a letter which I wrote to help Ross understand my feelings about what I considered to be a faulty decision process. This letter is also an example of how to use the, "I feel ... ," "Here's why ... ," "In the future please ... " technique in writing.

These letters and notes (and, by the way, they get letters and notes that praise also) help create an atmosphere of openness, understanding and fairness. Six years ago I would have just pouted about the incident and built resentment over it. Now I act.

Dear Ross:

I **feel** sorry that you decided not to take advantage of your second set of theatre classes.

Here's why I feel sorry. You had been asking for several months if you could attend some of these classes. You said they were really important to you and your developing interest in theatre. I called, got the information, and asked you what you wanted to do. After some thought, you decided to take these two classes.

There were no other dates for these classes and the biochick had not chosen her visitation times with you yet. You asked me to sign you up and pay for these classes, and I did.

"If I had to select one quality, one personal characteristic that I regard as being most highly correlated with success, whatever the field, I would pick the trait of persistence. Determination. The will to endure to the end, to get knocked down seventy times and get up off the floor saying, 'Here comes number seventy-one!'"

Richard M. Devos

10

> *"There are words which sever hearts more than sharp swords; there are words the point of which string the heart through the course of a whole life."*
>
> Frederika Bremer

When you changed your mind about them last week, it was a last-minute decision. Your earlier decision was based on several months of thought and action.

I feel that it is important for you to learn careful decision-making processes and to stick to the choices you make. The decisions you make that take time may be more important to your future learning than last-minute choices that simply seem to be fun at the moment.

If I am billed for this class that you changed your mind about, I will expect you to pay the $60. I am glad that I had only paid for one class in advance; otherwise, because of your last-minute change, I would have been out the other $60. You know that $60 is a lot of money, and right now we don't have much money in this house.

In the future, when you have made a careful decision about your activities, especially ones that involve money, I will expect you to stick to your original choice.

I want you to grow and learn well. I want you to be happy. Part of the learning process is planning ahead for learning and sticking to those plans. Summer learning times are especially important since they prepare you for your next school year.

Keep up your tape learning and book reading. I'll check with you to see how you're coming when I see you next.

How's the time- and self-management coming? Are you practicing it? I still have your time schedules from Washington D.C. I thought about you last week as I passed the White House and all the monuments! (I didn't see the President again, though. I guess you're just my good-luck charm!)

See you in a few weeks.

Love,

R-A

10

It's the Follow-Up with Those Eggs That Will Kill You

It's fairly easy to set standards. Making those standards stick is the tough part! Follow-up is my least favorite part of parenting. I just hate it when one of the kids breaks a rule or does not follow through. I don't like unpleasantness and, just like many of you, I view counseling as unpleasant. We'll be going along having lots of fun and really smooth waters, and then someone breaks a standard.

Careful monitoring and proactive coaching helps prevent the necessity of counseling quite so often. The eggs know, for example, that when Steve or I ask them to clean their rooms, there will be inspection before they are allowed to move to the next activity. The job description of room cleaning is already prepared, so what we do now is use this description as a checklist for performance evaluation. Did these things happen as agreed upon or not?

> *"It makes a great difference in the force of a sentence, whether a man be behind it or no."*
>
> Ralph Waldo Emerson

If all is well, inspection is passed, and we move on. If adjustments need to be made, adjustments are attempted, and then another inspection happens. This process goes on until agreed-upon standards are met.

If you skip the inspection, then the job must be completed satisfactorily, and another job from the list of family jobs is assigned.

Coaching often involves doing the job with the egg until she understands and assimilates the process. Yes, this is time consuming up front. The reward of doing this is that before long the job is accomplished without constant supervision and is done correctly. Don't assume that you have made it clear. Train for clarity. The amount of supervision and training necessary will vary by age and by egg.

Eggs need the order that sets them free to fly to all the heights they deserve to attain. Chicks and roosters are responsible for providing that order.

10

The Joys of Well-Disciplined Eggs

We have been working on this discipline issue for six years now. We began with incidents such as the retail-fixture-climbing incident I mentioned earlier. We progressed to one particularly memorable piano adjudication where we were waiting in the lobby of a very nice junior college for the results of Cam's performance. Two chicks and one rooster were watching three eggs climb all over the furniture; other chicks and roosters looked on in wonderment and dismay. I felt like a coward for being afraid to do in front of the biochick what I would have done instantly had I been with the eggs by myself.

I decided this would never happen again. I would have the courage to discipline whether there were ruffled feathers or not! That attitude and the willingness to say, "Not in this lifetime" have brought our nest to another plane of understanding and respect. Knowing that the rules were fuzzy was taken by the eggs as carte blanche to scramble the entire yard.

We just recently went to a party with all three eggs. The boys kept several adults in stitches listing, "Things You Never Say to a Stepparent." Stephanie was her cute, cuddly self and charmed everyone. My friend who hosted the party called me just a few days later. She said, "I just wanted to let you know how impressed all the people at the party were with your children. They can't stop talking about how well-behaved they were!"

We used to insist that the eggs stay with a babysitter if we were attending parties away from home. At home, eggs had to eat and play in the lower level while chicks and roosters enjoyed themselves upstairs. Those actions were taken because our training had not progressed to the point that we could trust the eggs to behave in ways that would not offend. Now, we love all being together in the same area. This was not just a part of the maturation process. It has come with the careful training, negotiation and cooperation of our nest team.

I have always had strict rules about where grains can be taken in the nest and where egg races can be held. At first, the eggs thought I was awful. Now they are proud of the way our nest looks because of the care and respect we have for it.

Discipline in school matters helped Cameron accomplish a perfect 4.0 eighth-grade school year. Because of that work, when

10

he transferred to a new school he was able to enter two honors courses and have a great head start on the study habits he would need to succeed in high school.

Cam has decided that he would like to go to West Point. His discipline in study habits will help him maintain the grades, activities and personal-development skills that will help him be accepted in a school of this quality.

Ross has built a flagging self-esteem through disciplining himself to develop study habits, healthy friendships and a budding talent as an artist. His artistic talent recently helped him solve a problem creatively. We had intended to finish his room in the lower level this past summer. At the same time, Steve decided to go into business for himself. This made dollars very tight in our house. Ross moved into an unfinished room.

The walls looked pretty naked in concrete color, and Ross and I sat down to problem-solve. We decided that he could paint the concrete wall entirely white. Then he can use it to paint art projects and graffiti to his heart's content. He went from being pretty disappointed about his unfinished room to excitement over the possibility of drawing on the walls! Remember my grandmother's saying, "You can get glad in the same pants you got mad in!"

Stephanie has progressed from being someone who had difficulty obeying rules to a person who problem-solves in a very adult way. I have always believed in having the kids create their own consequences, and she is more than fair in this area. She has learned to assertively go to the family member with whom she is having a problem and solve it directly with that person using the, "I feel ... ," "Here's why ... ," "Here's what I think is fair ... " method.

> *"In words are seen the state of mind and character and disposition of the speaker."*
>
> Plutarch

10

> *"When thoughts fail of words, they find imagination waiting at their elbow to teach a new language without words."*
>
> Anonymous

Chapter Summary: Am I Really Supposed to Do All of This?

This chapter has many suggestions and practiced techniques that will work for your nest. Don't try to use all of them at once. One at a time, beginning with the area of pain that your nest most often experiences, is the best way to start.

Communicating about "eggspectations" is a major factor in disciplinary success. This chapter's tools provide ways for chick and rooster to communicate, eggs to communicate with chick and rooster and the nest to achieve greater peace and success.

Eggs need the order that sets them free to fly to all the heights they deserve to attain. Chicks and roosters are responsible for providing that order. Allow your nest to experience joy together as you step up to parental responsibilities in a more positive way than ever before. It's not enough just to lay those eggs, they've got to be properly hatched!

"Some people regard discipline as a chore. For me, it is a kind of order that sets me free to fly."

Julie Andrews

C HAPTER 11

Protecting the Nest

"I don't get it. Do you?"

"The very difficulty of a problem evokes abilities or talents which would otherwise, in happy times, never emerge to shine."

Horace

"For everything you must have a plan."

Napoleon

Develop an Awareness of Legal Issues

One of the most difficult parts of trying to be a stepnest is the part that necessarily concerns legalities. I grew up in a very trusting family, where privacy was respected, and the law never seemed to be something that had any place in the life of a nest.

There were certain caveats of nest life I took for granted.

1. If someone promised something, promises would be kept.
2. No one in your nest would ever lie about you.
3. No one in your nest would ever cheat you.
4. No one in your nest would ever try to take advantage of you.
5. No one in your nest would ever manipulate you.
6. No one in your nest would ever try to take something that belonged to you.

11

7. Whatever you worked for and earned was absolutely yours.
8. Your nest respected your privacy and protected it with a vengeance.
9. No one in your nest would ever set you up.
10. You didn't have to be defensive because you could trust your nest and be open with them.

You may learn that the complicated feelings which are part of the stepnest can make each or all of these caveats untrue for the chickenyard. Within your nuclear stepnest, you can train and reinforce these truths. They may be true inside your own nest. They are often not true when applied to biochicks or roosters and exchicks or roosters.

You will learn, sometimes the hard way, that there are certain important issues you must be aware of, be proactive about and be prepared for. You are not an attorney. You have probably consulted several. This small chapter is included as an awareness opportunity for you.

It's not attempting to sound alarms, just to make you aware of some precautions. This chapter is not intended to remind you of negatives but to prevent situations from becoming negative and stressful. Many stepnests have not covered themselves in some important areas and have lived to regret and to pay through the nest. That regret and those checks that are written create stress even in nests that are successfully living together. The tension in the chickenyard after these "hits" is palpable!

Here are some issues, in no particular chronological order, about which stepchicks and roosters should be informed. Chickens with a head-in-the-sand attitude may choke on the sand. Relationships can be strangled, trust suffers and communication collapses.

Where dollar, time and liability issues are concerned, the stepchick or rooster **must** be and **has a right to be** informed. When your soon-to-be-spouse or current spouse doesn't want to share details, your welfare can be jeopardized and your future can be mortgaged. Communicate carefully and completely about these issues. Get your understanding and your spouse's understanding in writing for your communication benefit. We often misunderstand verbal information.

Above all, make no assumptions. You **must** communicate with your soon-to-be or current spouse about these issues:

Nest Legalities Communication Checklist

1. What are the terms of finances to the exchick or rooster?
    A. What are the terms of pending property sales?
    B. How is the asset liquidation being handled?
    C. What about retirement income?
    D. How have insurance agreements been taken care of?
        1. Life
        2. Health
    E. Who pays for private school?
    F. Who pays for college?
        1. Who pays tuition?
        2. Who pays for books, incidentals, living expenses?
    G. How long does any kind of support payment continue?
    H. Is there a provision for who buys cars?
    I. What about clothes, toys and other items needed at both houses?
    J. Is your spouse behind on child support?
    K. What if your spouse loses his/her job?
    L. What if your spouse becomes disabled?
    M. What are the income tax arrangements?
        1. Who takes deductions?
        2. Where are oldest and youngest children placed as deductions?
        3. Does the deduction status change at any time?
2. What are the agreed-upon living arrangements?
    A. Whose house will you be living in?
    B. What are the rules about moving out of state?
    C. How many days will the children be with you?
    D. Are there any unusual circumstances regarding custody or change of custody?
3. What are the communication terms?
    A. Through whom does communication and negotiation take place?
        1. The ex-spouses?
        2. Attorneys?

11

"I arise in the morning torn between a desire to improve the world and a desire to enjoy it. This makes it hard to plan the day."

E.B. White

> *"The house of everyone is to him as his castle and fortress."*
>
> Edward Coke

11

3. Mediators?
   a. If mediators are used, who chooses them?
   b. What enforcement power does the mediation process have?
   c. What are the advantages/disadvantages of mediation over court processes?
   B. How often does communication take place?
4. Can the stepparent's assets ever be counted in a renegotiation of child support?
   A. Know the law and precedent of your own state and the state where the divorce was obtained.
   B. If possible, before the marriage, take the necessary steps to protect the income you have and the assets you take into the marriage with you.
   C. Know how to protect your personal assets acquired even after the marriage takes place. (Unless you enjoy working to support the exchick or rooster, this is a very big issue.)
5. Ask to read the divorce decree.
   A. Be especially concerned with the parts relating to the eggs.
   B. Where do eggs go for holidays?
   C. What is the general tenor of the decree?
      1. Does it read like a marriage contract?
      2. Does it indicate the nature of the relationship with this exchick or rooster?
      3. Does it give you clues to the nature of the exchick or rooster?
   D. Picky points that seem unusual are clues.
6. Be aware of your liability responsibilities when the children are in your care alone.
   A. Do you have a limited power of attorney for medical care in an emergency?
   B. Are you able to take a child to the doctor for events such as sore throats?
7. How is your privacy protected?
   A. Can you be interrupted at your place of employment?
   B. Do your phone numbers have to be disclosed?
   C. How much of your financial circumstances have to be disclosed?
8. Do you have any legal rights as a stepparent?
9. Do you have any legal responsibilities as a stepparent?

This is in no way a complete list. Each circumstance will have issues in addition to these. This is a list to begin your thinking process. If you have been married for some time and some of these issues are ones you have not communicated about, this is a good time for clarification.

Knowledge is peace and security. Knowledge prevents resentment and surprise.

1. Protect yourself.
2. Protect your assets.
3. Protect the children medically.
4. Protect your spousal relationship.
5. Protect your stepfamily relationships.
6. Protect your stepfamily's financial future and security.

Do your own research. I was fortunate to have an attorney, Marilyn Shapiro, who was willing to guide me through the University of Missouri Kansas City Law Library. She got me started so well that it made it possible for me to save money by doing much of my own research.

I find that calls to attorneys for information and even some dollars spent on consulting fees are worth the mental strain of the "what-ifs" that occur when my income seems to be in jeopardy. I have worked very hard every day of my life since I was sixteen to put myself through school and to gather a financial present and future. I continue to work hard and want my income and assets to be distributed as I see fit. I choose for no one else to cash in on my hard work.

I am very generous with my stepeggs, and they will be the first to tell you this. I want to choose to be generous rather than have a court mandate that I must give the dollars not to them but to another chick who may choose how they are used.

Resentment and uncertainty present themselves to disrupt your stepnest when legal issues are not discussed and resolved. Injury and loss can occur when a stepchick or rooster is unsure of how to proceed in medical emergencies.

Protect the emotional, financial, and physical welfare of the nest. Be legally informed and proactive.

> *"I never said, 'I want to be alone.' I only said, 'I want to be* **left** *alone.'* **There is all the difference.**"
>
> Greta Garbo

11

217

?

11

Summary: Protecting the Nest

Use this worksheet mixed with your thoughts from this chapter to begin or continue thinking about nest protection. Forewarned is forearmed. Legal issues are unpleasant but ever-present stepnest nightmares. Turn those nightmares to proactive possibilities with some advance preparation.

Protecting the Nest Issues Worksheet

1. List of issues to discuss with spouse or spouse-to-be.

   _____

   _____

   _____

   _____

2. List of questions for my attorney.

   _____

   _____

   _____

   _____

3. List of issues to research in the law library.

   _____

   _____

   _____

   _____

"Now, in the exacting twilight, to choose, not what we shall do or how we shall live but to choose the life whose dreams will hurt least in the nights to come."

Yehuda Amichai

CHAPTER 12

Bonding, Empowering and Celebrating in the Nest

"Do you believe this?"
"Will you look at us?"

"If you take any activity, any art, any discipline, any skill, take it and push it as far as it will go, push it beyond where it has ever been before, push it to the wildest edge of edges, then you force it into the realm of magic."

Tom Robbins

"The need for devotion to something outside ourselves is even more profound than the need for companionship."

Ross Parmenter

We're in This Nest Together: Let's Make Magic!

In our nest, we do a lot of planning, working, playing and celebrating successes. We don't wait for big successes and big projects; we work, play and celebrate as each opportunity presents itself. Magic is in the eye of the nest beholding it. We choose to make magic as often as possible.

One Saturday the kids and I had a unique opportunity to create magic. We were going to have the whole day to ourselves. Steve was at a sales meeting, and our work was done. We really had a free day, and we could choose how to spend it!

Friday night we began planning. Planning works really well for us because then we know what to expect and find that our happiness increases when expectations are met. We discussed several options and decided to begin our day by walking two miles to get bagels at our favorite bagel store.

> *"I believe people will do their best, provided that they are getting proper support."*
>
> Debbie Fields

12

Saturday morning we had a glorious day for a walk. Sun shining everywhere, late May, early Saturday morning, the whole day before us, who could ask for more? Ross and Stephanie decided to roller skate rather than walk. Cameron and I mildly attempted to warn them that with shoe skates, if they decided they didn't like the skating, they were going to be stuck with this option. We tried to tell them that skating would be harder than walking.

They maintained that the skating would be easier. I wasn't entirely certain one way or the other, and I didn't want to begin on a negative note so I told them, "Just realize that you are stuck with this decision."

About a mile into the skate/walk, all the kids were tired, but the skaters were obviously bushed and resting frequently. It had become a very hot, humid day. I tried to think of ways to "think ourselves out." We imagined air conditioners, swimming pools and being sprayed with cold hoses.

That worked only briefly, and then I tried teasing. "I'm older than all of your ages put together, and I'm not griping." The kids' point of view was that made it easier for me. We made up games and contests to try to make it fun. We barely made it to our destination.

Once we got to the bagel bakery, one by one the kids sneaked off to try to call Steve, hoping that he had come home early and would rescue us from the return trip by picking us up. When all phone attempts failed, and, after eating, drinking and being refreshed, we began our trek home.

We stopped at the grocery store to get refreshing drinks. Again, we tried to call Steve as we rested in the welcome shade of the grocery-store canopy. This was becoming a major exercise in on-the-spot motivation and encouragement. By now all three kids were whining and exhausted.

As we left the grocery store, I had to invent more "thinking out" exercises, encourage the depressed and kick the mental behinds of the most discouraged. At one point, Stephanie decided that she was going to throw up. (She had already tried whining, crying, threatening and begging. She had even tried to get Cam to trade shoes with her!)

I said, "You are not going to throw up! Take five deep breaths." With Steph, the key to success is making it sound scientific. If I had just said, "Breathe deeply," she wouldn't have taken it seriously. When I said "five," she believed it was a real remedy and tried it. She didn't throw up.

About this time (one block from home), Dad had returned and "rescued" us. He had heard our calls for help on the answering machine.

We really needed to "save" this experience, so we decided to build pride in our accomplishment. We immediately retraced our steps traveling in the van with the trip meter set. We had walked exactly 5.0 miles. Everyone cheered up instantly and became proud of this achievement.

We issued certificates of accomplishment and instituted the "Five Mile Club." To maintain membership, we take other walks for fun and fitness. What an opportunity for teaching and bonding. Here's a copy of our certificate:

"He found him in a desert land, and in the howling wilderness; he led him about, he instructed him, he kept him as the apple of his eye."

Deuteronomy 32:10

Certificate of Membership in the

FIVE MILE
CLUB

Issued to

STEPHANIE
CLURMAN

Issued on July 31, 1993
for courageous walking!

Issued by proud parents...

_____

_____

To bond, you must spend time together. The kids keep their certificates on their desks and still talk fondly and jokingly about that Saturday morning.

Nest Bonding Through Sports Activities

One of our fun activities in the summer is baseball. Cameron has played since he was nine and Stephanie began when she was ten. One summer we decided the team needed encouragement so Steve and I appointed ourselves team cheerleaders. We developed a list of **Parent Support Opportunities** and **A COMET Champion's Checklist**. We'll be happy to share these with you because the spirit among the families of that team was the best we have ever experienced.

COMET Parent Support Opportunities

1. Surprise "Pep Rallies"
    A. Gather before a game to:
        1. Provide a special motivational treat such as:
            a. "I'm a Comet" sweatbands
            b. "Chew 'em up" notes attached to bubble gum
        2. Post good-luck banners in the dugout.
        3. Cheer as the team comes on to the field.
        4. Wear "We love Comets" shirts.
    B. Gather after a game to:
        1. Provide treats.
        2. Show support.
        3. Go to a special restaurant for a victory party.
    C. Provide yard-sign decoration:
        1. After the team is chosen
        2. Before a big game
        3. Before a tournament
        4. Before an away tournament
    D. Create a personal pep rally.
        1. Pair the team members on paper.
        2. Each team member delivers a special support message to his partner the day before the game.
            a. Card
            b. Good-luck piece such as:
                1. Lucky penny
                2. Lucky socks

12

      3. Lucky sweatband
    c. Yard banner
E. Have a car rally.
    1. A group of parents decides to personally deliver treats to each team member's home before a tough game as extra support.
    2. Parents go house to house in vans/cars to pick up the team early the evening before a game and take them out for pizza.

Here's the Champion's Checklist.

A COMET Champion's Checklist

How to beat myself.

1. Know my PPB (Previous Personal Best)
    A. Create a Challenge Chart.
        1. List my own stats.
        2. Check each one off as I beat it.
        3. Challenge myself with a new personal best.
        4. Keep my own chart up to date before each game.
    B. Create a Chore Chart.
    Based on my stats and my coach's recommendations, create a practice schedule for myself.
        1. Skill I am working
        2. Number of days a week to work on it
        3. Number of repetitions
        4. Who could help me/coach me?
        5. Place to practice
        6. Time to practice (day/time)
    C. Create a Champion Chart.
    What are my championship strengths?
        1. What do I think my strengths are?
        2. What does my coach think my strengths are?
        3. What do my parents think my strengths are?
        4. What do my teammates think my strengths are?

12

> *"Never one thing and seldom one person can make for a success. It takes a number of them merging into one perfect whole."*
>
> Marie Dressler

2. Help a Teammate Beat Himself.
    A. Study the stats of two teammates.
        1. List two teammates you would like to study.
        2. What do you think her strengths are?
        3. What does he think her strengths are?
        4. What does the coach think her strengths are?
    B. What can you do to help your teammate beat her PPB?
    C. List two things you can do as her teammate in the next game which will support this teammate.
3. Beat the Opposition.
    A. Study the opposition.
        Ask yourself/your coach these questions before each game. Ask in time to give your team a chance to study the opponent.
        1. What do you know about this team?
            a. How many games have they won?
            b. Who's the best infielder?
            c. Who's the best outfielder?
            d. Who's the best batter?
            e. What's the pitcher's style?
        2. What do we need to do to win when playing this team?
        3. What strengths do the Comets have that will help us defeat this team?
        4. What are the two most important things to remember when playing this team?
    B. Study the opposing coach.
    C. Carry yourself in a professional way to scare the opposition and gain their respect. (Fake it till you make it!)
        1. When you make a mistake, don't let it show on your face!
        2. When you return to the dugout, don't throw helmets, gloves, bats or do anything to show you feel you haven't done your best.
        3. Walk with confidence when returning to the field.
        4. Walk with pride when stepping up to bat.
        5. Walk with pride when returning from an at-bat.

The night before one of the biggest games, Steve and I made signs that said, "Home of a COMET" and staked them on each team member's home lawn. We had so many comments and thank

"Persistent people begin their success where others end in failure."

Edward Eggleston

12

yous and expressions of pride from coaches, parents and kids that we felt really rewarded by what we had decided to do.

Just noticing what the eggs are doing that they feel good about and participating in the activities important to them change the way nest members feel about each other.

One summer we decided to have our own family baseball camp. We ran it very professionally. Steve has operated a camp of sorts every summer since then. Now this camp extends as a training program that reaches throughout the entire year. Physical fitness has become a nest bonding experience.

Nest Bonding Through Religious Activities

Our church attendance has been another great bonding experience for us. Anything that we do together on a regular basis helps us have shared history. Building shared history is one of the most important things that a stepnest can do to bond.

When Cameron was confirmed, we planned a special weekend. We gave him special attention, cards, gifts and time. Attending church or synagogue together:

A. Models a life-support skill
B. Reinforces home- values teaching
C. Bonds by creating Saturday and Sunday routines
D. Establishes common values/experiences

We created a special plaque for Cam. Here's the text of it:

> *"When love and skill work together, accept a masterpiece."*
>
> John Ruskin

12

> ***Cameron Clurman***
> God's child (loved by God)
> Our child (loved by Dad and Ruth-Ann)
> Our brother (loved by Ross and Stephanie)
> Welcome to the part of God's family called
> Grace Covenant Presbyterian Church.
> Congratulations on completing
> a very important part of your life.
> We are proud of you through sticking it out through
> Confirmation Class.
> We are happy you have found this experience meaningful.
>
> ***We love you, Cam-Clur!***
> 5/22/94

12

Bonding Through Special Stepnest Celebrations

We celebrate our stepfamily anniversary. We either prepare a meal together at home or make a trip to a favorite restaurant. We decide whether we want to be casual or formal and plan it in advance to make it special.

Our "Hanumas" celebration is one we look forward to all year. Steve is Jewish, and the rest of us are Presbyterian. We needed to create a special celebration for our unique circumstances. Ross begins asking about Hanumas in March and starts bugging me in September. He reminds me that the night before Thanksgiving is special because that's when we always decorate the Hanukkah bush and the Christmas tree.

We have nights of candle blessings during Hanukkah and a potato latke festival. After the potato latkes we all go to look at the Christmas lights. Our blended cultures have made a rich and unique tradition that we each treasure and anticipate. Celebrating holidays by creating special nest times and traditions:

   A. Creates fun times together
   B. Creates "things I can count on"
   C. Creates stability and security

The uncertainty of some nests can create instability and insecurity in eggs if you don't overbalance those feelings with traditions and things you do every week that are the same.

Summary: The Importance of Egg Empowerment

Life lessons are a part of what you are supposed to learn as a member of a nest. Home is the beginning of learning. You learn how to hatch, how to be parent chicks and roosters, what character is, how to hatch into a disciplined, responsible and likable adult chick or rooster.

I take every opportunity to teach. I learned from years of classroom experience with teenagers that this pays off and eggs write and call years later to thank you for your help.

I also came from a family with parents and grandparents who never missed a chance to teach. I learned things that I remember and live by such as:

- Be clean (inside and out).
- Pick yourself up by your own bootstraps.
- Cheaters never prosper.
- You can get glad in the same pants you got mad in.
- What's the minus on the "A" for?
- Never do it the easy way just because it's easy.

I had wonderful parenting and wonderful grandparenting. I am thankful for my models and use them in my own parenting. What are some of the things I teach? On our walk we learned endurance, thinking out, responsibility (carry your own skates!) and coping strategies. The teaching shows my eggs I care about them. They tease me about it, and they appreciate it. They also think I'm sick or depressed if it doesn't happen. In a recent essay for his English class about his grandma (he picked my mom to write about), he said, "She raised my stepmom well. I can tell because my stepmom is strict and is raising us well."

> *"One can never consent to creep when one feels an impulse to soar."*
>
> Helen Keller

12

> *"Courage and perseverance have a magical talisman, before which difficulties disappear and obstacles vanish into thin air."*
>
> John Quincy Adams

Planning activities which involve togetherness, play and learning have been our best opportunities to bond. Anything good has a price. Belonging and bonding are good. To achieve them, you have to plan and follow through. When your stepegg comes up, hugs you and says, "You're the best stepparent in the whole world," you'll fly above the yard for hours.

CHAPTER 13

Something to Crow About

"We got it, so get it!"
"We got it, so get it!"

"Change is the only thing that offers new opportunity."
Ross Shafer

The Advantages of Living in a Stepnest

"Life asks not merely what can you do; it asks how much can you endure and not be spoiled."

Harry Emerson Fosdick

13

Your society does not tell you that living in a stepnest has any advantages. The disadvantages are outlined quite specifically. You have probably had the experience of reading newspaper articles, magazine articles, association publications and books on stepnests which caused you to feel that yours was a doomed nest. Your eggs were not only going to be cracked but pecked to bits and jailed. Your renewed attempt to build a new nest would result in even greater disaster than the previous attempt.

Worse yet, the yardbirds are constantly squawking about what a mistake you have made and why in the world did you do this to yourself? There are positive, affirming stepnests. You just never hear about them. For some reason, it's much more lucrative to write and talk about failure in stepnests than success.

I have known many people who were and are in stepnests who are wonderful individuals, not on drugs, not in jail, not dismal failures. I have known many second marriages much more successful than the first. All the information I was reading was saying that stepfamilies will produce delinquents and second marriages were more likely to fail. I rebelled against all the negatives I was reading. How could our nest defy this information and be successful? How could our nest produce evidence and information to enhance our own success and help other stepnests to be successful?

Let's Look for Some Productive Stepnest Evidence

My own father was a member of a stepfamily. A warmer, more wonderful example of a human being you could never find anywhere. Ward H. Lawrence's life alone was testimony to me that stepnests could produce loving, caring, sensitive individuals.

As a pastor noted for his loving pastoral care, he was loved by members of his church congregation. As a father, each one of his four children will swear to you that no better father could be found on earth. As a son and older brother, his family loved and respected him. Even Army buddies, college friends and seminary colleagues kept in touch with him for years after World War II, asking his counsel and valuing his friendship. I knew that if my own father was such a success as a person, there had to be hope for stepnests.

There is good news and hope for the type of nest which statistics tell you will be the most common type of nest by the year 2000. As I searched out stories, examined the strategies our nest has used and began to listen to eggs, chicks and roosters in stepnests, I discovered two main things:

1. Parenting is always a challenge, no matter the nest type.

2. Twenty-first century parents have got to step up to bat, not hide in the dugout.

Neither biochicks and roosters nor stepchicks and roosters can parent by default. Parenting must be a conscious choice.

13

Create Your Own Nest Success Evidence

To get yourself and your nest to begin thinking about the advantages of life in your nest, try some of these exercises together. (This will also help you produce evidence when other significant yard members and the media try to tell you how sad it is that you have to live the way you do!)

Things Our Nest Can Crow About

1. Make a list of things stepchicks and roosters and eggs experience with deeper feeling (such as compliments and praise from each other).

   _____

   _____

   _____

   _____

   _____

2. Construct a list of nest successes.

   _____

   _____

   _____

   _____

   _____

3. Create your own list of advantages to living in your stepnest.

   _____

   _____

   _____

   _____

   _____

13

4. Create a list of good things in your life that would not have happened if you had not been in this stepnest.

_____

_____

_____

_____

_____

5. Write some special things that happen in your stepnest.

_____

_____

_____

_____

_____

6. List your favorite moments in your stepnest.

_____

_____

_____

_____

_____

7. Write one thing you really appreciate about each member of your stepnest.

_____

_____

_____

_____

When You Don't Think the Sky is Falling, It Won't

How can living in a stepnest be advantageous in the 21st century? How can eggs, chicks and roosters learn life skills that will benefit them in the business world and help them be happier in their personal lives? As you have read this book, I hope these advantages have been apparent to you. I hope you will talk about these advantages with the chickenyard at large. You need to read these in newspapers, hear about them on talk shows and reeducate your yard to the positives. The negatives are not absolutes.

"You must look into people as well as at them."

Chesterfield

Advantages of Life in the Stepnest

1. **Stepnests learn constructive responses to change.**
   A. Change in stepnests is usually immediate.
   B. Change in stepnests is a constant.
   C. It's OK that we are sometimes happy and sometimes unhappy.
   D. Constructive response to change is character building.

2. **Stepnests must learn teamwork to thrive and survive.**
   A. Creative problem-solving works best with a team approach.
   B. Nest teams learn that using a piece of each egg, chick and rooster's idea contributes to the greater success of the team.

3. **Stepnests learn to work "across departments."**
   A. Different nest environments work together for successful egg gathering.
   B. Eggs have ample opportunity to see what happens when "departments" choose to work together or fight each other.

4. **Diversity is an everyday challenge and can be mastered.**
   A. There are advantages to being made aware of different lifestyles and cultures.
   B. It is possible to adapt and live comfortably in very diverse nests.
   C. Some nests are easier, more comfortable and more enriching to live in than others. (You need to choose the nest that is best for you!)
   D. There is richness in diversity.
   E. It's OK that nests are different.

13

> *"Human improvement is from within outward."*
>
> Froude

5. You can hold true to your own values even when living in an environment where values are different from yours.
   A. I need to know what is important to me.
   B. I need to know what I value.

6. You can agree to disagree.
   A. Nestmates and nests who have very different ideas can cooperate to achieve a goal.
   B. I do not have to like you for each of us to be successful.

7. Nestmates who initially dislike each other can discover ways to respect each other.
   A. Respect can replace dislike.
   B. Like can come after respect.
   C. Sometimes love comes after like.

8. Goal-setting reaps satisfying rewards.
   A. Stepnests need to work harder to succeed.
   B. Hard work reaps benefits.
   C. After initial groundwork, things get much easier and much more peaceful.

9. Individuals are unique, not difficult.
   A. Each person can remain true to himself and be a valuable, contributing member of the nest team.
   B. You do not have to be clones or even from the same gene pool to work together.

10. Out of failure and brokenness can come success and wholeness.
   A. One broken relationship does not mean chicks and roosters are incapable of forming successful nests.
   B. Eggs can observe an example of a successful chick and rooster relationship that can help them feel better about and provide a model for successful chick and rooster relationships of their own.

11. The objectivity of the stepchick or rooster can be helpful to everyone.

Summary: You Can Choose to Be a Successful, Supportive Nest

> *"Talent is nurtured in solitude; character is formed in the stormy billows of the world."*
>
> Goethe

As a stepnest, you can choose to reject the notion that you are throwaway eggs, chick and rooster and the result of fractured nests. You can choose instead to be an example of the resiliency of the human spirit.

Pressure can produce power or pain. You choose.

As a stepchick or rooster, choose to experience this unique kind of parenting with surprise and wonder. Know what you have worked through in your family. Remember the times when it wasn't fun and you hid out in your bedroom. Value those moments when your eggs:

- Take your hand in a shopping mall.

- Put a head on your shoulder in church.

- Send you a Mother's or Father's Day card.

- Are disappointed when work calls you away from home.

- Look forward to seeing you at the end of a school day.

- Are eager to plan activities that you do together.

- Enjoy just "hanging out."

- Tell you "secrets" about their friends and experiences.

- Comfort you when you are sad.

- I challenge each stepparent to dare to parent.

13

> *"Only what we have wrought into our character during life can we take away with us."*
>
> Humboldt

I challenge each stepparent to:

1. Be the adult.
2. Get over the resentment.
3. Risk the rejection.
4. Work toward the day when you can say with me:

"I love these children! They bring joy to my life. They add a dimension to living that I would not have missed for the world. I thank God for them. I want the best in life to come to them. Working with them, I will help them be responsible, happy, loving, likable human beings."

13

State of the Nest
Report Card

Do you know your neighbor in the nest?

KNOWLEDGE EVALUATION

Scale   1   2   3   4   5   6   7   8   9   10

      Low   Moderate   High

(I know what my partner   (I don't know what my

would say about this.)   partner would say about this.)

Report Card Directions: Rate each point of knowledge on where you are as you begin reading this chapter. Do this exercise individually. Compare notes after finishing the exercises in Chapter One.

1. The most important responsibility of a parent

2. Your partner's parenting style

3. The thing your partner liked least about his/her ex-spouse

4. The thing your partner liked most about his/her ex-spouse

5. The type of discipline in your partner's childhood family

6. The thing your partner liked least about the way he/she was raised

7. The thing your partner liked most about the way he/she was raised

8. The way my partner likes to celebrate birthdays

9. The way my partner likes to celebrate holidays

10. The type of relationship my partner wants to have with his/her ex-spouse

11. The things my partner would like to change about his/her divorce agreement

12. The manners that are important to teach children

13. How important religion/faith are to my partner

14. My partner's four most important values

15. How my partner shows anger

16. How my partner wants me to show emotional support

INDEX

YOUR BACK-OF-THE-BOOK STORE

Order Form

Because you already know the value of National Press Publications Desktop Handbooks and Business User's Manuals, here's a time-saving way to purchase more career-building resources from our convenient "book store."

• IT'S EASY ... Just make your selections, then mail, call or fax us your order. (See back for details.)

• INCREASE YOUR EFFECTIVENESS ... Books in these two series have sold more than a million copies and are known as reliable sources of instantly helpful information.

• THEY'RE CONVENIENT TO USE ... Each handbook is durable, concise and made of quality materials that will last you all the way to the boardroom.

• YOUR SATISFACTION IS 100% GUARANTEED. Forever.

60-MINUTE TRAINING SERIES™ HANDBOOKS

TITLE	RETAIL PRICE	QTY.	TOTAL
8 Steps for Highly Effective Negotiations #424	$14.95		
Assertiveness #442	$14.95		
Balancing Career and Family #415	$14.95		
Change: Coping with Tomorrow Today #421	$14.95		
Customer Service: The Key ... Customers #488	$14.95		
Empowering the Self-Directed Team #422	$14.95		
Getting Things Done #411	$14.95		
How to Conduct Win-Win Perf. Appraisals #423	$14.95		
How to Manage Conflict #495	$14.95		
How to Manage Your Boss #498	$14.95		
Listen Up: Hear What's Really Being Said #4172	$14.95		
Managing Our Differences #412	$14.95		
Master Microsoft® Word #406	$14.95		
Motivation and Goal-Setting #4962	$14.95		
A New Attitude #4432	$14.95		
PC Survival Guide #407	$14.95		
Parenting: Ward & June ... #486	$14.95		
Peak Performance #469	$14.95		
The Polished Professional #426	$14.95		
The Power of Innovative Thinking #428	$14.95		
Powerful Leadership Skills for Women #463	$14.95		
Powerful Presentation Skills #461	$14.95		
Real Men Don't Vacuum #416	$14.95		
Self-Esteem: The Power to Be Your Best #4642	$14.95		
SELF Profile #403	$14.95		
The Stress Management Handbook #4842	$14.95		
The Supervisor's Handbook #410	$14.95		
Team-Building #494	$14.95		
Techniques to Improve Your Writing Skills #460	$14.95		
The Windows Handbook #4304	$14.95		
The Write Stuff #414	$14.95		
Supreme Teams:--How to Make Teams Work #4303	$14.95		
Fear & Anger --Slay the Dragons That Hold You Back #4302	$14.95		

Business User's Manuals — Self-Study, Interactive Guide

TITLE	RETAIL PRICE	YOUR PRICE	QTY.	TOTAL
The Assertive Advantage #439	$26.95			
BEING OK JUST ISN'T ENOUGH #5407	$26.95			
Business Letters for Busy People #449	$26.95			
Dealing with Conflict and Anger #5402	$26.95			
Hand-Picked: Finding &-Hiring ... #5405	$26.95			
High-Impact Presentation and Training Skills #438	$26.95			
Learn to Listen #446	$26.95			
Parenting the Other Chicks Eggs #5404	$26.95			
Prioritize, Organize: Art of Getting It Done #453	$26.95			
The Manager's Role as Coach #456	$26.95			
The Memory System #452	$26.95			
Taking AIM On Leadership #5401	$26.95			
Sex, Laws & Stereotypes #432	$26.95			

SPECIAL OFFER: Orders over $75 receive **FREE SHIPPING**		
Subtotal		$
Add 7% Sales Tax *(Or add appropriate state and local tax)*		$
Shipping and Handling *($1 one item; 50¢ each additional item)*		$
Total		$

VOLUME DISCOUNTS AVAILABLE — CALL 1-800-258-7248

Name_____ Title _____

Organization _____

Address _____

City _____ State/Province _____ ZIP/Postal Code_____

Payment choices:

❑ Enclosed is my check/money order payable to National Seminars.
❑ Please charge to: ❑ MasterCard   ❑ VISA   ❑ American Express

Signature X _____ Exp. Date_____ Card Number _____

❑ Purchase Order # _____

MAIL: Complete and mail order form
with payment to:
National Press Publications
6901 W. 63rd St.
P.O. Box 2949
Shawnee Mission, KS 66201-1349

PHONE:
Call toll-free **1-800-258-7248**

FAX:
1-913-432-0824

Your VIP No.: 705-008438-096